刘墉给孩子的汉字启蒙书

（美）刘墉◎著/中文·图
（美）刘轩 （美）刘倚帆◎著/英文

北京联合出版公司
Beijing United Publishing Co.,Ltd.

图书在版编目（CIP）数据

刘墉给孩子的汉字启蒙书：汉、英／（美）刘墉，
（美）刘轩，（美）刘倚帆著；（美）刘墉图. -- 北京：
北京联合出版公司, 2019.8
ISBN 978-7-5596-3349-1

Ⅰ. ①刘… Ⅱ. ①刘… ②刘… ③刘… Ⅲ. ①汉字—
儿童读物—汉、英 Ⅳ. ①H12-49

中国版本图书馆CIP数据核字（2019）第112787号

《刘墉给孩子的汉字启蒙书》，经刘墉授权在中国大陆地区独家出版发行。

刘墉给孩子的汉字启蒙书

作　　者：（美）刘墉　（美）刘轩　（美）刘倚帆

图：（美）刘墉

责任编辑：李　伟

北京联合出版公司出版
（北京市西城区德外大街83号楼9层　　100088）
北京盛通印刷股份有限公司印刷　　新华书店经销
字数170千字　　700毫米×980毫米　　1/16　　21.5印张
2019年8月第1版　　2019年8月第1次印刷
ISBN 978-7-5596-3349-1
定价：68.00元

谨以此书献给——
谢济群和许碧华两位老师，
谢谢她们的热心教学
为刘轩和倚帆打下良好的中文基础。

This book is dedicated to Chi Chun Hsieh and Bi Hwa Hsu,
two teachers whose enthusiastic tutelage
gave Xuan and Yvonne a solid foundation in Chinese.

◆ 引言│Introduction

认识各体汉字，发掘文字起源，欣赏书法之美，探寻趣味典故，学习中英文，增添生活乐趣，立即学以致用！

Learn Hanzi etymology, appreciate calligraphy in its various forms, discover the origin of Chinese characters and the stories behind them, and find their use in daily life!

◆ 目录｜Table of Contents

◆ 一个字、一张画 、一个故事

A character, a picture, a story

多半的人小时候学写汉字，都觉得挺辛苦。

Most people who learned to write Chinese characters when they were young, remember it as a difficult task.

可不是吗？拼音文字只要会说，大概就能八九不离十地拼出来。汉字却一笔一画、左撇右捺，简直像画画。不过顺着这条路想，如果小孩学汉字的时候，都能用游戏的心情去画，不是很有意思吗？

And difficult it certainly was! Alphabetic writing systems can be learned in a logical way; if you can pronounce it, you can probably write it. But Chinese characters are drawn one by one, stroke by stroke, like miniature paintings. Though it seems laborious, if we follow this line of thought and let children treat Chinese as a drawing game, wouldn't it make the whole task of learning much more fun?

譬如先画个框框，里面再画个小女孩，是形容女娃娃的"囡"；框框里面画个人，那人则成为关在里面的囚犯。

For example, first draw a box frame, then draw a little girl inside. That is the character "囡", which means "a little girl". But if inside the frame you draw an adult person "人", the character "囚" means "a prisoner".

两扇门当中画个太阳，是中间的"间"；换成一个人，是一闪而过的"闪"。

The sun "日" in the middle of double doors "门" makes "间", which means "between". If you change that sun to a person, it makes "闪", meaning "a flash". You can imagine a person appearing in the doorway in a flash.

月亮还没下去，太阳已经从草坡上露脸，是黎明的"朝"；太阳不但落进草地里，还落了又落，落下两个太阳，是"暮"。

The moon has not disappeared, but the sun has already risen from beyond the grassy slope: that is the character "朝", which means "dawn". When the sun not only falls into the grass, but continues to fall, appearing as two suns in a double image, it becomes "暮", meaning "dusk".

把"口"里的东西吐到"土"上，是"吐"；从"天"上掉东西到"口"里，是"吞"。

From the "mouth" "口" onto "earth" "土" makes "吐" meaning "to spit"; from the "sky" "天" into "mouth" makes "吞", which means "swallow".

也有些字很抽象，譬如，上面写个"中"，下面画只手，正好抓住上面"中"的那一竖，是必须公正执中、不偏不倚的"史"；上面写个中，下面画个心，是把良心放在最中央的"忠"。

Some characters are also abstractly expressive. For example, if you write "middle" "中" on top with a hand on the bottom grasping the vertical stroke of the "中", it makes "史", which means "history". A hand writing something that is "balanced and impartial" seems to suggest the ideal of historical writing. If you write "中" and put a heart under it, that yields the character "忠", which means "loyalty". You can think of it as "loyalty is where you put your heart at the center".

往复杂一点看：草莽的"莽"，笔画虽然多，其实很简单：上面是草，下面也是草，中间一只狗在跑，不是很荒野、很草莽吗?

Let's look at a more complex character, such as "莽". Although the character has many strokes, it is actually very simple when you think about it as a picture: there is grass above, there is grass below, and a dog "犬" is running between the grass. Is it not a very "wild" "grassy" image?

还有跳蚤的"蚤"，好像挺复杂，其实只要画一只手，在手指间画一个像跳蚤的小点子，下面再加个"虫"字，就成了。至于流水的"流"，只要在左边画三点水，右边画个长头发、头朝下的"子"，好像一个人在水里游泳就对了！

There is also the character for flea "蚤", which seems quite complicated at first glance. In fact, just draw a hand and a small dot like flea between the fingers, then add the radical for insect "虫" below, and there you have it! As for the character "flow" "流", draw three splashes of water on the left side, three strokes resembling long hair on the right side, and a "child" "子" with his head down, as if swimming in the water.

以上都是这本书里介绍的汉字，它们经过我的挑选，让小朋友和初学汉字的外国人能够很快进入汉字的王国。这个入门非常重要，一个人如果从一开始就用图画的方式学习汉字，这可以影响他一生。因为死记硬背学的汉字是死的，从图像入手学的汉字是活的。好比你新认识一个人，起初只知道他的名字，但是如果有一天，那人邀请你去他家，你知道了他的家庭背景，甚至人生遭遇，下一次见到他，他虽然还是那个样子、还叫那个名字，但在你心里，他却变得"亲切"了。

These are the Chinese characters introduced in this book. They have been selected by me so that children and foreigners who are learning Chinese can quickly enter the land of imagery and imagination. This entry is very important. If a person learns characters this way from the start, it can influence the rest of the learning process. Chinese characters that are rote memorized are dull, but Chinese characters learned from imagery come alive. It's like getting to know a new friend. At first you only know his name, but if one day, the person invites you to his home, and you learn about his family and his life story, next time when you see him again, even though he still looks the same and you call him the same name, he will feel "friendly" to your heart.

这本书是我和儿女合作的。儿子早年到美国才读小学一年级，女儿则是在美国出生的，为了让他们不忘本，我坚持教他们中文。儿子因为在中国学过一年，还好教些，女儿就难了，因为她生长在美语环境下，为了让她不排斥学汉字，我不得不设计一套"从图画到剪影到文字，外加生活照片"的方法。而且为了让她知道汉字是怎么演变成今天的样子，我会把甲骨文、大篆、小篆、隶书、行书和楷书都写给她看。又为了确定她懂了，我在用中文解说之后，总要她翻译成英文，并且鼓励她说：将来可以出书。

This book is a collaboration with my children. My son Xuan lived in the United States since his early years, and my Yvonne daughter was born there. In order to educate them on their roots and culture, I insisted on teaching them Chinese myself. My son had his early education in China, so he already had the fundamentals, but my daughter was a different story. In the American environment, for her to accept learning Chinese characters, I had to design a system that taught her the characters as a set of pictures, from drawings to sketches to text, with the addition of photos from real life. And in order to let her know how Chinese characters have evolved into what they are today, I wrote out the oracle bone, big and small seal, clerical, semi-cursive and cursive versions of the scripts, all the way to the present-day regular script. And to make sure she truly understood, I always asked her to translate my explanations into English. I even encouraged her efforts by saying, "One day, we can publish this as a book!"

二十多年后的今天，我的诺言终于实现了。因为女儿翻译的时候年纪小，英文比较稚嫩，我还请刘轩做最后的校正，借机让儿子又温习了一次。太太则担任中文校对和与出版社的联系工作，真可以说是全家联手的作品。

Today, more than twenty years later, my promise has finally come true. Because Yvonne was younger when she did the original English translation, I also asked Xuan to make the final edits. He said it was a good opportunity to refresh the material. My wife Weiwei did the proofreading and corresponded with the publishing house. It was a true family effort.

这本书的编辑工作，主要是我今年暑假在中国台北完成的，为了找到能够配合的照片，我常常不得不顶着烈日出去拍摄。正在澳洲度假的儿子和在纽约工作的女儿也被我隔海催稿，我们决定把在台首版版税全部捐作公益，以感谢读者几十年来对我们的爱护！

　　The editorial work of this book was mainly done in Taipei this summer. In order to shoot suitable photos for the characters, I often had to venture out with my camera in the hot noon sun. My son who was on vacation in Australia, and my daughter who is working full time in New York, have also been "drafted" by me on short notice to complete this manuscript. Finally, we have decided as a family to donate all the royalties from the first Taiwan edition for social benefit, as gratitude for the many years of love and support we have received from readers like you. Thank you all!

刘墉　二〇一八年七月

Yung Liu, July 2018

◆ 这本书的使用方法
How to use this book

这本书是通过图画、剪影和各种字体介绍汉字的演进。

This book introduces the etymology of Chinese Hanzi characters through illustrations, cutouts and various written forms of a character throughout history.

它能改变你看汉字的态度，让学写字不再是刻板的功课而是生动的艺术，让每个汉字不再只是符号，而成为看图说故事。

Learning Chinese characters in this way becomes less of a chore and more like art. A character is no longer a symbol but an illustrated story.

更有趣的是，在每个汉字之后都有一张在世界各地拍摄的照片，让你像是寻宝般在里面找出刚学的那个字，使文字立刻跟你的生活融合。

In addition, each character is accompanied by photographs taken from around the world. You can search for the character in its environment, thus making a connection between the character and what you see in daily life.

请看下面的例图：

For example:

HOW to use THIS BOOK

第一页

这一页是个楷体字和它的注音，你可以先打开这一页，猜猜这是什么字。

Page 1:

The introduction to each character opens with a page of the character in regular complex script, together with its phonetic spelling in zhuyin and pinyin forms. You can use this page as a flashcard to test yourself in the future.

第二页

这一页的上方是以生动的彩色图画表现字的源头，下方则是很浅白、易懂的中英文解说。

Page 2:

This is a color illustration showing the pictographic meaning of the character, followed by a simple explanation.

【 mǎng 】

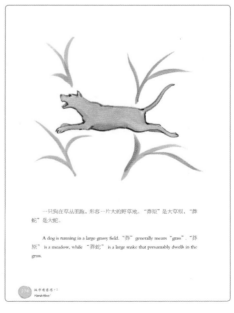

一只狗在草丛里跑，形容一片大的野草地。"莽原"是大草原，"莽蛇"是大蛇。

A dog is running in a large grassy field. "莽" generally means "grass". "莽原" is a meadow, while "莽蛇" is a large snake that presumably dwells in the grass.

第三页

这一页的上方是与第二页相对应的剪影，它可以让大家很自然地把图画和文字联想在一起。下方从左到右介绍那个文字从甲骨文、大篆、小篆、隶书、行书到楷书的演变。
（第 323 页到第 339 页还有各种字体的中英文解说。）

Page 3:

Top of this page is the illustration from page 2 transformed into a silhouette. This acts as a visual "bridge" between the illustration and the written forms of the character. On the bottom of the page, from left to right, shows the character, s evolution through history, from oracle bone script to regular script. An extended introduction to the various script forms can be found on pages 323–339.

第四页

一张彩色照片，拍自世界各地与中文有关的一些地方。新教的字藏在一堆招牌或风景里，请读者小心地找出那个字。这样做既有寻宝的趣味，又能让大家把刚学的字带到生活当中，养成很好的学习态度：在生活中学习！学习用在生活！

Page 4:

Here is a photograph taken from various locations where Chinese characters can be seen. The character you have just learned will be somewhere in the pho－ tograph. By looking for it like an Easter egg hunt, you can link the word with its naturally appearing context. Learning from daily life and putting that into use is certainly the best attitude to have when learning Chinese characters!

汉字有意思！
Hanzi Alive !

朝

【cháo】 【zhāo】

　　我们常能看见太阳已经出来了，月亮还没落下去。把太阳和月亮放在一起，是不是也能表示早上呢？

　　可以！但是要表现太阳还在草里，没有完全升起，这就是"朝"字的由来。日本最大的报纸《朝日新闻》，就取了"朝"和"日"作报纸的名字，意思是每天早上出的报纸。

　　"朝" means "early morning", because at dawn, we can still see the moon while the sun is rising. So when you put the sun and moon together, can it also mean "dawn"?

　　Yes! However, the sun must be shown to be in the grass because it has not yet fully risen. Japan's largest newspaper《朝日新闻》has the words "朝" and "日", meaning that it is a newspaper which comes out every morning.

剪影

甲骨文　金文　小篆　隶书　行书　楷体

一起找一找

朝：摄于美国佛州迪士尼世界橱窗。

【mù】

学了"早"，你或许要问，傍晚该怎么写？

太阳西落时不是也落在草上吗？与"早"有什么不同呢？

中文字里是有不同的，它不像"早"，把太阳画在草上，而是画在草当中，表示太阳落到草里去了。后来，不知为什么又加了一个太阳，成为今天的"暮"字。

After learning "morning" "早", you might ask, "How do you write 'dusk'?"

When the sun sets, doesn't it set in the grass also? Then what is the difference between the two words?

Unlike "早", where the sun rises over the grass, the sun in "dusk" "暮" has already set into the grass. Later, for reasons not known to us, another sun was added to make the current character for dusk: "暮".

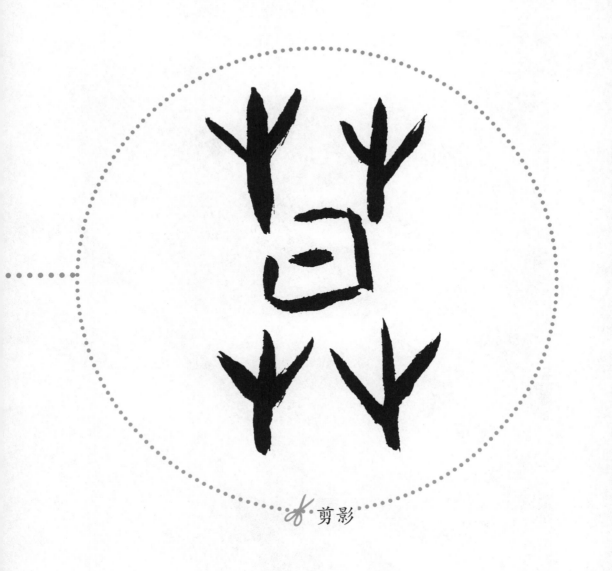

剪影

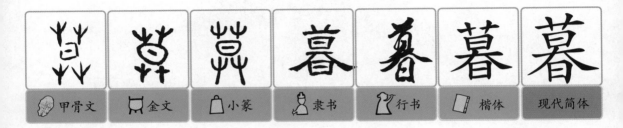

甲骨文　金文　小篆　隶书　行书　楷体　现代简体

【nú】

　　"女"字的右上方，有个像叉子的"手"。用手指挥女人做事，这个字是"奴"。（在封建时代常常歧视女性，造成许多贬义词跟女性有关，请大家谅解！）

The pictograph on the right has a fork-like symbol that resembles a hand. A hand ordering a woman to work becomes the word "奴", meaning "slave". (In the feudal era, women were often discriminated against, causing many derogatory words related to women. Fortunately we are moving out of such backward thinking in modern Chinese society.)

剪影

【fù】

婦【繁体】

这个字虽然看起来像"奴"，但是在"手"的下面多加了一个"𠬶"，成为"妇"（婦），意思是拿着扫帚的女人。如果只写"手"和那个扫帚，不加女字边，则是扫帚的"帚"。

This character looks like "奴", but there is a "𠬶" under the hand "手", forming "妇"（婦）, meaning "married woman", or a woman holding a broom. If you leave out the "女" in "婦", the word becomes "帚", meaning "broom".

剪影

甲骨文	金文	小篆	隶书	行书	楷体	现代简体

【nān】

一个"女"孩睡在娃娃床里，是幼女的意思，在中国有些地方的人管女儿叫囡（nān）。

A girl sleeping in a crib, means "little girl". People in some parts of China still refer to their daughters as "囡", pronounced as "nān".

剪影

| 甲骨文 | 金文 | 小篆 |  隶书 | 行书 | 楷体 |

一起找一找

图：摄自刘墉著《小姐小姐别生气》封面。

劉墉著

小姐小姐别生氣

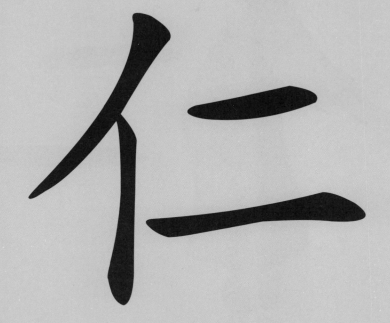

【rén】

　　在"人"的旁边加两横，表示人与人之间应该有的态度，这是中国儒家最讲求的"仁"。

　　Adding two lines next to "人", represents the ideal of interpersonal conduct. This is "仁", translated as "benevolence" or simply as "humanity", is the most highly regarded of the Confucian principles.

剪影

甲骨文　金文　小篆　隶书　行书　楷体

41

一起找一找

仁：摄于中国台北迪化街。

【jiān】

上面写个"小"字，下面写个"大"字，是"尖"。

Writing "小"（small）on top of "大"（big）or something small on top and something big on the bottom, makes "尖", which means "sharp".

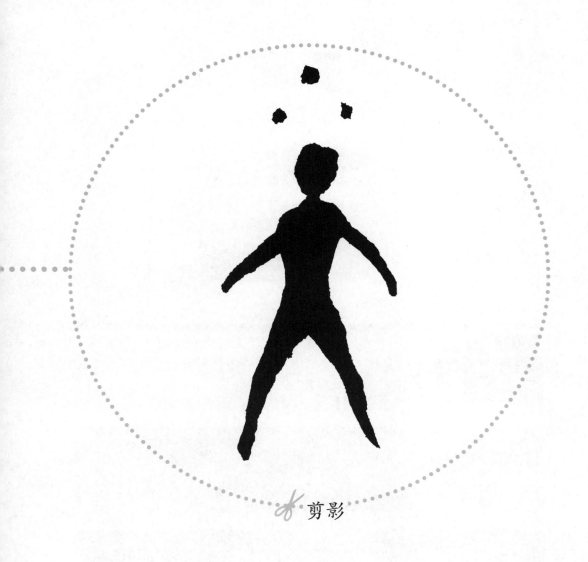

剪影

| 甲骨文 | 金文 | 小篆 | 隶书 | 行书 | 楷体 |

一起找一找

尖：摄于中国北京。

【yāo】

虽然像个"大"字，但是头垂向一边，是"夭"。意思是短命。

This character looks like "大", but its head is drooping to one side. This is "夭", meaning "short life".

剪影

甲骨文　金文　小篆　隶书　行书　楷体

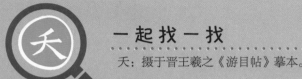
龍跳天門虎
卧鳳閣

石渠寶笈藏右軍快雪帖為法書之甲丁
勾歲復得是帖筆法圓勁入神如游龍天
矯非鉤摹家所能彷彿末有遽去齋跋云
載入書譜中真蹟何妨視快雪帖弛難為
伯仲矣乾隆戊辰首夏御識

有鍾紹京書印二字小印
鍾蓋唐之越公也晉謝奕
謝安桓溫三帖上并黄
素黄庭經上俱有此印
見米元章寶章待訪錄
而黄庭經今藏韓冑州
慶予屢見之无可疑證
守和審定
耳

魏
泰

【yāng】

把"大"放在"П"的正中间，是"央"，也就是"中间"的意思。中国人常用"中央"形容正中间。

Putting "大" in the middle of "П" makes "央" meaning "center". The word "中央" means "central" or "central authority".

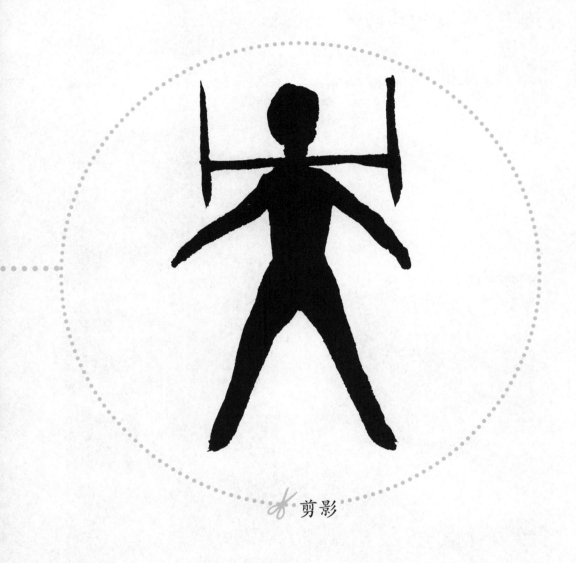

剪影

| 甲骨文 | 金文 | 小篆 | 隶书 | 行书 | 楷体 |

一起找一找

央：摄于中国北京。

【 wèi 】

在"立"字旁边多加个"人"，成为一个正面和一个侧面的人，但只有正面站着的人脚下有一横，表示他有"站的地方"。这个字是"位"。

汉语称"一个人"为"一位"，"两个人"是"两位"。管坐的地方叫"座位"。"个"跟"位"都是量词，但是"位"比"个"感觉上来得尊敬。

Adding a "人" beside "立" depicts one person facing the viewer and another person facing sideways. Only the person facing the viewer has a horizontal line under his feet, to show that he has a place to stand. This character is "位" meaning "spot" or "place".

In Chinese, one person is quantified as "一位"; two people are quantified as "两位"; one's seat is "座位". Like the character "个", "位" is a quantifier. Both can be used to refer to numbers of people, but "位" is a more respectful word in regular usage.

剪影

甲骨文　　金文　　小篆　　隶书　　行书　　楷体

57

專用
停車位
Disabled Parking Only

【jiā】【jiá】【gā】

夾【繁体】

一个大人的两臂撑开，左右各夹一个小孩，是"夹"（夾）。

凡能塞进东西的，都可以说是"夹"，譬如"皮夹""档案夹""发夹"。

An adult's arms are spread with a child under each arm. This is "夹" （夾）meaning "to clamp". Any object that can clamp other objects can be called "夹". For example: 皮夹（wallet, literally "leather clamp"）, 档案夹（folder, literally "file clamp"）, and 发夹（hair clip）.

 剪影

甲骨文	金文	小篆	隶书	行书	楷体	现代简体

一起找一找

夹：摄于中国北京。

放夹子

【 qiú 】

　　一个人被框起来，好像被保护，但是跟"囡"不一样，它不代表小女孩，而是指监狱里的囚犯，意思是一个被关起来的人。

　　You may think that a man in a frame is being protected, but that's not the case here. "囚" actually means "a prisoner".

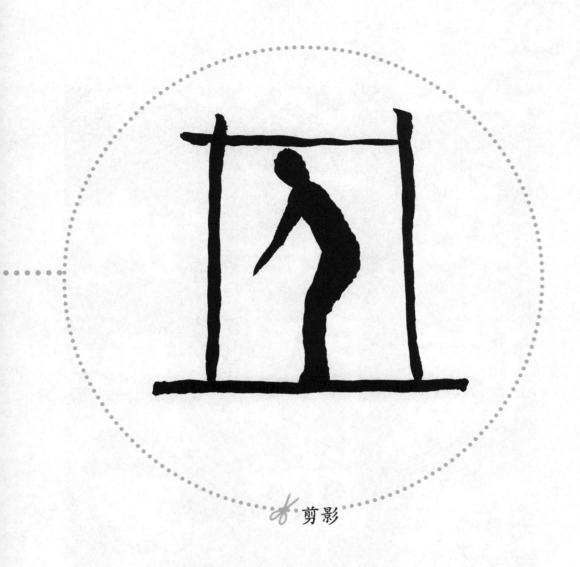

剪影

甲骨文　　金文　　小篆　　隶书　　行书　　楷体

65

一起找一找

囚：《张迁碑》拓本。

从

【cóng】

從【繁体】

　　这个好像一个人跟着另一个人走的字，是"从"。作为动词，它的意思是"跟随"，作为介词，它的意思是"来自"。

　　This character "从" looks like one person following another. As a verb, it means "to follow", and as a preposition, it means "from".

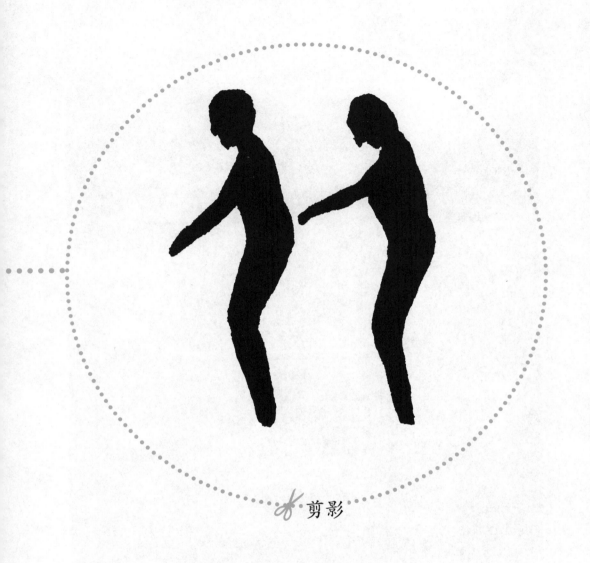

剪影

| 甲骨文 | 金文 | 小篆 | 隶书 | 行书 | 楷体 | 现代简体 |

一起找一找

从：摄于中国北京。

安全提示

水面(冰面)危险，请勿游泳(滑冰)、禁止向水面(冰面)丢垃圾。
龙形水系水源为再生水，请勿饮用、放生及垂钓。
为了您的生命及财产安全，请到正规娱乐场所从事水上娱乐项目。

【dǎ】

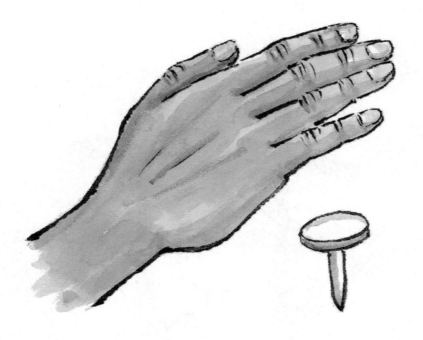

用手去敲钉子，是"打"。打仗、打架、打球、打拳都用"打"字，如果把我们前面学过的"人"放在"打"的后面，就成了"打人"。

A hand hitting a nail is "打", which means "to hit". This character can be combined to form many words. For example: "打仗" = "battle", "打架" = "fight", "打球" = "play ball"（literally "hit ball"）, and "打拳" = "boxing" （literally "hit fist"）. What do you think "打人" means?

剪影

甲骨文　金文　小篆　隶书　行书　楷体

一起找一找

打：摄于新加坡。

星海南雞

STAR HAINANESE CHICKEN

歡迎打包
Takeaway.
Hotline

FIVE STAR KAMPONG CHICKEN

WELCOME

【 běi 】

　　相反地，两个人朝相反的方向行走，就是"背"了，也意味着意见不合，相违背；又因为很早以前，当时所谓的外族，常从北方侵入中国，所以"北"也指北边。

　　Two people walking in opposite directions is "背", which can mean "backside"（背面）. It can also mean disagreement or contradiction（违背）. Historically, since invaders of ancient China often came from the north, the character for "north" is now also "北".

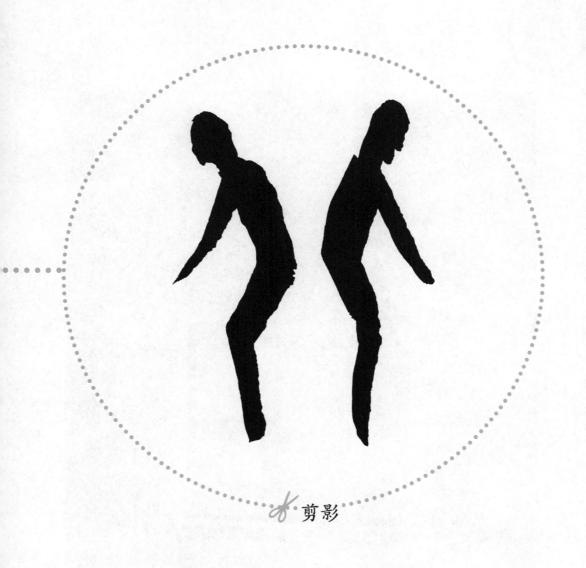

剪影

甲骨文　金文　小篆　隶书　行书　楷体　现代简体

一起找一找

北：摄于中国北京长城。

北京市文物保护单位

万里长城北京段

慕田峪

北京市人民政府一九八四年五月二十四日公布
北京市文物事业管理局一九八四年九月立

【bài】 【bái】

　　两只手合在一起是"拜"，中国人见面行礼，常常用"拜"来代替握手。中国人管结婚叫"拜天地"，向神明行礼祈福，叫"拜拜"。

Putting two hands together makes "拜", which means "to worship". Instead of shaking hands, Chinese may put their hands together in this way when greeting each other. "To worship heaven and earth" "拜天地" is a saying referring to "the act of marriage". Going to temple to worship and give offerings is "拜拜".

剪影

| 甲骨文 | 金文 | 小篆 | 隶书 | 行书 | 楷体 |

保儀大夫 〔植福宮〕

福德正神俗稱土地公，曾任朝廷稅官，王母令八仙化作為乞丐，往生得年若，年二月初二出生，一出生，王母令八仙化作為乞丐，容貌不變，福德圓滿，往生得年若，年二月初二出生，至終生八十一歲，誠心修持，福德圓滿，更是隆擬聞事終局，凡為人向善之土地之神，掌管大地之財。凡為人向善，財富豐宜，掌管大地之財，和氣生財，祂亦是古代的牙人為來買管轄該區城之土地、財運亨通，和氣生財，祂亦是古代的牙人為來買祂不謹是社稷之神，主張買賣雙方應以和為貴，更是隆敦厚善良生意神之介人，主張買賣方應以和為貴，敦厚善良生意順利，財運亨通，每月初二及十六日皆有祭祀牙神，尤以農曆二月初二之「頭牙」及十二月十六日之「尾牙」，更是隆重祭祀。

民間祭祀之土地公神像，令人望生無限期待，企求一生福祿雙全，故土地又篤實的員外臉龐，慈祥瞇眼的微笑，滿臉白髮，重視祭祀。

公是善男信女的希望。

保儀大夫，張公諱巡，唐朝鄧州南陽人，博覽群籍，深通戰陣，滿面翻幹，書讀經三過，即能背誦，終生不忘。開元末進士及第，授太子通事舍，後派任清河、真源二縣令，為官清廉，政績卓著。天寶年間，安祿山造反，賊勢大潰散。公率吏民哭拜玄宗皇帝廟，起兵討賊，以少敵眾，積大小三百餘戰。睢陽被賊城，太守許遠告急於公，公即入睢陽與許合兵，救為河南節度副使堅守孤城，賊傾眾邊城，被圍數月，且糧盡援絕，乃掘鼠捕雀以食，鼠雀盡，乃出愛妾供士食，城陷罵賊，齒皆破裂，睢陽軍民數萬人，朝廷嘉公等忠義，救封公為保儀大夫均成仁取義，並無降賊。朝廷嘉公等忠義，以昭忠烈。遠為保儀尊王，建忠順廟，同饗廟食，以昭忠烈。

本島歷年遭受蝗蟲災害，農民無以為計，詣廟禱告，或某像到災區繞境，農害蕩然不復為災，保儀大夫等香火鼎盛，社甚

【 shòu 】

　　一只手给东西，一双手接过，是"授"，意思是给予。譬如"授权""授予学位"，这些比较慎重的赠予，汉字常用"授"来表示。

This character's meaning is "to grant". The character shows one hand providing, and a pair of hands receiving. Words that can be formed with "授" include "授权"（to grant authority），"授予学位"（to grant a degree）. The character refers to a more formal type of giving.

剪影

| 甲骨文 | 金文 | 小篆 | 隶书 | 行书 | 楷体 |

一起找一找

授：摄于中国台北实践大学。

【xiū】

  人靠着树，是"休"，就是休息。商店如果在门上挂个"休"字，就表示休业，暂时不对外营业。

  A person leaning against a tree is "休", meaning "to rest". If you were to see this character outside a shop, it would mean that the shop is currently not open for business.

剪影

甲骨文　金文　小篆　隶书　行书　楷体

一起找一找

休: 摄于日本。

【gè】【gě】

　　如果只画三片竹叶，意思是一枝竹子，也就是"个"。这个字后来笔画变多了，如今繁体写成"個"。个是汉语中最常用的量词，譬如"一个人""三个女人"。

We have just introduced the word "竹", which is a character showing two sets of bamboo leaves. But what if we only write one set of bamboo leaves? There would be "only one", or "个". "个" has no specific meaning on its own, but it's one of the most frequently used quantifiers. For example, "一个人" means "one person", "三个女人" means "three women".

剪影

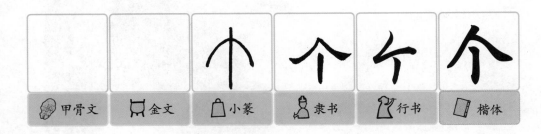

甲骨文	金文	小篆	隶书	行书	楷体
		巾	个	乞	个

一起找一找

个：摄于中国北京。

【 shǐ 】

　　上面写"中"，下面加一只手，正好抓住中间那一竖，表示用手拿笔，写不偏左也不偏右的事，这"公正"又"公平"的写作，就是"史"。写历史不是都该公公正正、不偏不倚吗？

　　"中"　means　"middle". Adding a hand under　"中", implies writing about things that are unbiased, neither leaning left nor right. This character　"史"　means　"history". Ideally, historical records should be unbiased and balanced, right?

剪影

甲骨文　金文　小篆　隶书　行书　楷体

【zhōng】

　　如果把一个"中"字放在心的正上方，意思是在心中、在心的最中心，也就是忠实、忠心的意思。

　　"心中"和"中心"，意思不一样，"心中"是心里面，"中心"是正中央。

If "中" is placed directly above a heart, it would mean "in the middle of the heart", or in other words, "loyal and faithful".

When writing "中" and "心" as separate characters, the order of the characters makes a difference in the meaning; "心中" means "in the heart", while "中心" means "center".

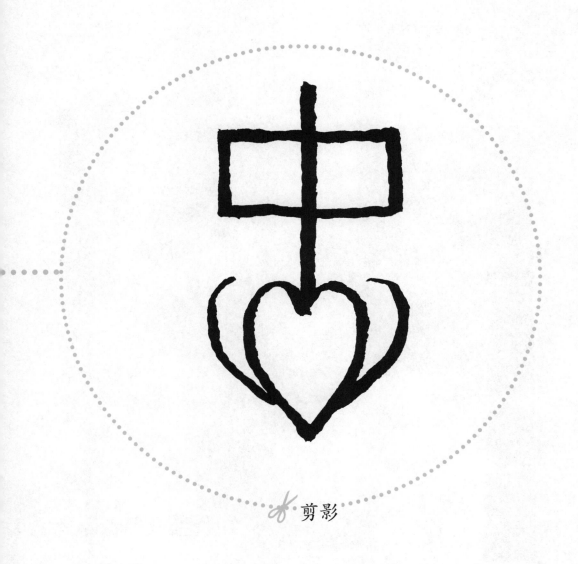

剪影

甲骨文　金文　小篆　隶书　行书　楷体

一起找一找

忠：摄于泰国曼谷。

【 zhòng 】

左边放个"人"，右边放个"中"，意思是在人与人之间。

"仲"有"在人与人之间介绍"的意思，譬如你想买房子，可以去"房屋中介"，那"中介"就是介绍人。有时候也可以称作"中人"，也就是"中间人"。

"人" on the left with "中" on the right makes "仲", which means "between people".

"仲" can also mean "to refer or to introduce people". For example, if you wanted to buy a house, you would go to a "房屋中介" or a "house introducer". "中介" means broker in this case or "one who introduces". It is sometimes also referred to as "中人", which can be understood literally as "middleman".

剪影

甲骨文　　金文　　小篆　　隶书　　行书　　楷体

一起找一找

仲：摄于中国香港。

【jiè】

　　一个人站在中间，左右各画一个小点，表示在"二者之间"。小点渐渐发展成在人下面加两画。汉语说"介绍"时用"介"；在二者中间协调事的人叫"中介"。

　　另外有一种说法是：甲骨文"介"字左右两个小点形容披在身上的铠甲，所以有壳的水中动物也叫"介类"。

One person stands in the middle with dots on either side, symbolizing "between two people" .This gradually developed into two strokes below the person. The Chinese phrase for introduce is "介绍"; a mediator is "中介人".

Another interpretation of the oracle bone inscription is that the two small dots represent armor on a person. By the same logic, shellfish（fish with armor）are called "介类".

剪影

甲骨文　金文　小篆　隶书　行书　楷体

一起找一找

介：摄于中国台北。

【 xiōng 】

　　上面写"口"，下面写"人"，并不是"人说话"，而是指可以先说话的人，那是谁? 是哥哥，汉字写成"兄"。

Here is a character with a mouth on top and a person on the bottom, but it doesn't just mean "a person talking". Instead, it is meant to represent "the person who has the right to talk first". Who is that? It is "the elder brother", which is the meaning of this character "兄".

剪影

甲骨文　金文　小篆　隶书　行书　楷体

所謂「福由心造，禍在己為」，命運是由個人的心念、作為所決定的：如果人人能一日三省吾身，知錯能改，且經常照顧好自己的身、心、口，善念匯聚，自然累積成一股浩然正氣，上達天聽，人間就能平安祥和。

禍福無門 惟人自召

人心轉處天心轉

願天下無災無難，讓我們從己身「三業」做起。

——淨身、淨心、淨口

淨身：「行好事」，不結惡緣。「五倫」就是善之源，為人處事，愛家庭，朋友及社會，就能遠離乖戾之氣，而擁有平安的生活。

淨心：「做好人」，不起惡念。智慧的人寬大、善解，內心不起貪愛、嗔恨及執著，才能常保清淨自在。

淨口：「說好話」，不造口業。一句好話莊嚴自己，鼓勵別人，口不出妄言、謊言與惡言，自能享有好人緣。

奉行五倫八德

五倫

君臣有義
父子有親
夫婦有別
長幼有序
朋友有信

八德

孝——敬順長輩
弟——友愛兄弟
忠——大公至正
信——誠正信實

禮——節制規範
義——行事合宜
廉——高風亮節
恥——勇於改過

願大家虔誠修身、修心、修口 祈求平安

行天宮 與您共修

【 zhòu 】

　　在"兄"旁边再加一个"口"，意思是在拜神时由哥哥带头，向神明祈祷，这个字是"咒"。

Adding another mouth "口" to the character "兄" makes "咒", which means "incantation". It symbolizes "the eldest son leading the family in worship".

剪影

		呪	呪	呪	咒
甲骨文	金文	小篆	隶书	行书	楷体

【zhān】【zhàn】

　　这个字也与拜神有关，上面那两画是"卜"，表示用甲骨算命时，在龟甲或兽骨上呈现的裂纹。巫师凭裂纹来说吉凶，就是"占"。中国人算命常说"占卜"。

　　The top part of this character is "卜", which symbolizes the cracks on tortoise shells, a common method of divination in ancient China. Adding a "口" to that makes this character "占", which means the act of divination, also written as the phrase "占卜"。

剪影

甲骨文　金文　小篆　隶书　行书　楷体

一起找一找

占：摄于中国台北。

葱油餅

姓名占卜專家

百吋大銀幕

風

加　啡

公司行號
墓見
手相
會名
面相
黃鐵斗數
八字流年
百事諸斷

命理數
靈體共修
風水鑑定
制化煞收驚
擇日祈福
開北安神

預約專線

本棟8F之10

現：中華易學研究會顧問
任：台北市易經學會命理主講教師

【tǔ】【tù】

　　"口"和"土"放在一起，表示从口里把东西吐到地上。这就是"吐"字。

　　This character puts mouth "口" and dirt "土" together, which is "to spit" something on the ground.

剪影

| 甲骨文 | 金文 | 小篆 | 隶书 | 行书 | 楷体 |

全民健康保險緊急傷患急診條件

一、急診定義：凡需立即給予患者緊急適當之處理，以拯救其生命，
　　　　　　　縮短其病程，保留其肢體或維持其功能者。

二、適用範圍如下：

　（一）急診腹瀉、嘔吐或脫水現象者。

　（二）急性腹痛、胸痛、頭痛、背痛、（下背、腰脇痛）、關節痛或牙痛、
　　　　需要緊急處理以辦明病因者。

　（三）吐血、便血、鼻出血、咳血、溶血、血尿、陰道出血或急性外傷出血者。

　（四）急性中毒或急性過敏反應者。

　（五）突發性體溫不穩定者。

　（六）呼吸困難、喘鳴、口唇或指端發紺者。

　（七）意識不清、昏迷、痙攣或肢體運動功能失調者。

　（八）眼、耳、呼吸道、腸胃道、泌尿、生殖道異物存留或因體
　　　　阻塞者。

　（九）精神病患有危及他人或自己之安全，或呈現精神疾病症狀須

　（十）重大意外導致之急性傷害。

　（十一）應立即處理之法定或報告傳染病。

　（十二）生命徵象不穩定或其它可能造成生命危急症狀者。

【tūn】

　　"口"和"天"放在一起，表示有东西从上面进入口中。这是"吞"。

　　Mouth "口" and sky "天" together symbolize something entering the mouth from up above. This character is "吞", meaning "to swallow".

剪影

甲骨文	金文	小篆	隶书	行书	楷体

129

【shuān】

閂【繁体】

　　两扇门中间，加一根横的棍子，使门从外面打不开，是"闩"（閂），也是锁的意思。中文说"闩门"，就是把门锁上。

Putting a bar across a set of double doors will keep the doors from opening. This is "闩"（閂）, which means "to lock". The phrase "闩门" means "to lock the doors".

剪影

| 甲骨文 | 金文 | 小篆 | 隶书 | 行书 | 楷体 | 现代简体 |

一起找一找

闪：摄于中国北京。

凤头部·第二章 ... 37

余姥姥道："有一种刑罚，名叫'阎王闩'，别名'二龙戏珠'，不知当用不当用。"

王大人道："快快讲来听听。"

余姥姥便把那"阎王闩"的施法，细细地解说了。王大人听罢，喜笑颜开，道：

"你们先回去准备着，待本官奏请皇上批准。"

余姥姥说："制造那'阎王闩'，甚是麻烦，就说那铁箍，硬了不行，软了也不行，需用上等的熟铁，千锤百炼后方好使用。京城里的铁匠没有一个能干了这活。望大人宽限些时日，让小的带着徒弟，亲自动手制作。俺们那里什么都没有，各种器械都靠着小的和徒弟们修修补补将就着使用，还望大人开恩，拨些银子，小的们好去采购原料……"

王大人冷笑着说：

"你们卖腊人肉给人当药，每年不是能捞不少外快吗？"

余姥姥慌忙跪到地上，你爹我自然也跟着跪在地上，姥姥说：

"什么事也瞒不过大人的眼睛，不过，制造'阎王闩'是公事……"

王大人道："起来吧，本官拨给你们二百两银子——让你们师徒赚一百两吧——这活儿你可得尽心尽力去做，来不得半点马虎。宫里太监犯了事，历朝历代都是由慎刑司执刑；皇上把任务交给刑部，这事破了天荒。这说明皇上记挂着咱刑部，器重着咱刑部，天恩浩荡啊！你们一定要加小心，活儿干得俊，让皇上高兴，怎么着都好说；活儿干丑了，惹了皇上不乐意，砸了咱刑部的招牌，你们的狗头就该搬家了。"

我和余姥姥胆战心惊地接受了这个光荣的任务，欢天喜地地支取了银子，到护国寺南铁匠营胡同里，找了一家铁匠铺，让他们照着图纸，打造好了"阎王闩"上的铁头箍，又去了骡马大街，买了些生牛皮，让他们编成皮绳，拴在铁头箍上。满打满算，花了四两银子还不到，克扣下白花花的银子一百九十六两多，给王大人养在精灵胡同里

【 jiān 】【 jiàn 】

間 【繁体】

　　门打开，中间有个太阳，意思是"在当中"。这个"间"（間）字可以形容位置，譬如"中间"；也可以形容时间，譬如"日间"。很早以前，门中间也可能是"月"，后来才确定用"日"。至于中间是月亮的"閒"则代表悠闲。

　　A sun "日" appear in the middle of a set of doors "门" means "in the middle of". This character "间"（間）can be used to describe a position, such as "中间", which means "middle". It can also describe a time, such as "日间" meaning "daytime". Originally, a moon "月" between a set of doors can also mean "in the middle of", but since then we have settled on "间" being the definitive version of this character. The moon version "閒"（pronounced xián）has come to mean "leisure".

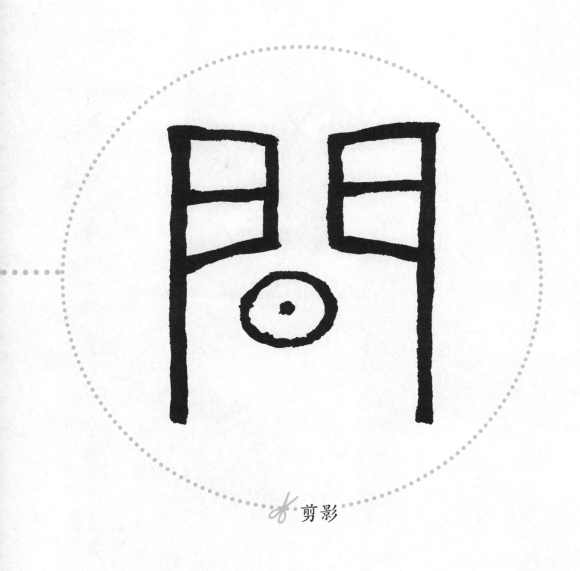

剪影

甲骨文　金文　小篆　隶书　行书　楷体　现代简体

一起找一找

间：摄于中国北京。

【 xián 】

閑 【繁体】

　　门外不见日，也不见月，看到的是一棵树，多美啊！它是"闲"
（閑），跟"閒"意思一样，都很悠然。

　　A tree "木" seen through a set of doors "门" depicts a relaxing view. This character "闲"（閑）means "idle" or "leisure". It is synonymous with "閒" which shows a moon through double doors, also a leisurely and relaxing sight.

剪影

| 甲骨文 | 金文 | 小篆 | 隶书 | 行书 | 楷体 | 现代简体 |

一起找一找

闲：摄于中国北京。

【kāi】

開【繁体】

两只手把门闩拿起来，是"开"，这意味着"开放"。

Two hands removing the bar from the lock （门闩）is "开", which means "to open".

剪影

| | 甲骨文 | 金文 | 小篆 | 隶书 | 行书 | 楷体 | 现代简体 |

一起找一找

开：摄于中国北京。

【guān】

關【繁体】

　　两只手用绳子或锁链把门绑紧，是关（關）；在古铜器上见到的"关"（關）看起来像是两只手正在把门掩上。

This character "关"（關）means "to close". It shows two hands tying a door closed with rope or chain. On ancient bronzeware, "关"（關）appears as two hands covering a door.

剪影

| 甲骨文 | 金文 | 小篆 | 隶书 | 行书 | 楷体 | 现代简体 |

149

一起找一找

关：摄于中国北京。

【shǎn】

閃【繁体】

　　有个人影在门口一闪，不见了，这个字是"闪"（閃）。"闪"是"很快"的意思，譬如"躲闪""闪电"。

This character "闪"（閃）means "flash". You can imagine it as a person appearing "in a flash" in the doorway. Some words made with "闪" include "躲闪"（to hide）and "闪电"（lightning）.

剪影

		小篆	隶书	行书	楷体	现代简体
甲骨文	金文					

153

【 mēn 】【 mèn 】

悶【繁体】

　　把心关在门里，多闷哪！这个字是"闷"（悶）。心烦是闷，空气不流通也是"闷"。

　　To hide your heart behind closed doors, how depressing! This word is "闷"（悶）. A troubled heart is "闷", but it can also mean "to seal tightly" or "stifle".

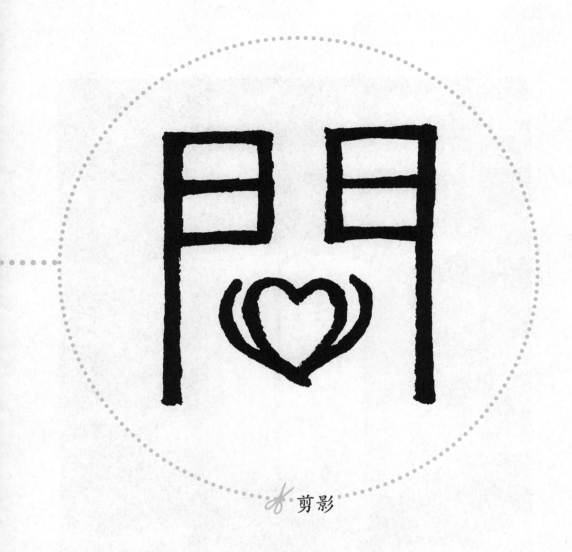

剪影

甲骨文	金文	小篆	隶书	行书	楷体	现代简体

一起找一找

闷：摄于中国北京。

【wén】

聞【繁体】

　　门中间有个耳朵，意思是听，汉语管最新的消息叫"新闻"，又说"百闻不如一见"。

　　有意思的是，当汉语说"闻一闻"的时候，不是"听一听"，而是"嗅一嗅"。

A ear within a set of doors, looks like eavesdropping, doesn't it? This character "闻" means "to listen". The word "新闻"（literally "newly heard"）means "news".

There is another saying, "百闻不如一见", which means "hearing about something a hundred times doesn't beat seeing it once". However, when the Chinese say "闻一闻", they don't actually mean "take a listen", but rather "take a whiff（to smell）"! It is a peculiar distinction, but an important one to remember.

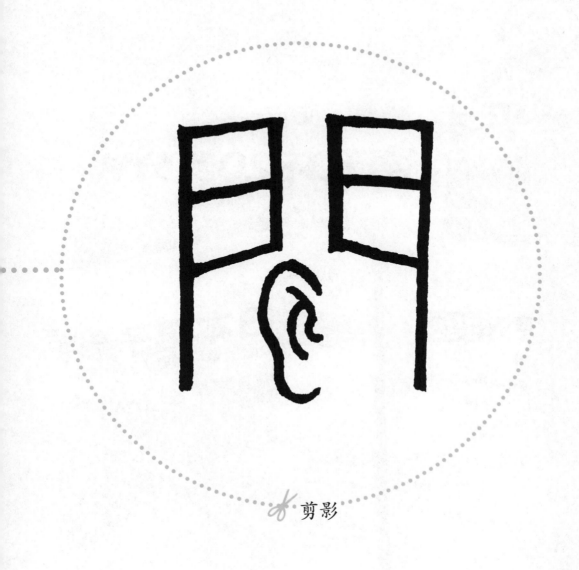

剪影

闻

一 起 找 一 找

闻：摄于中国北京。

平本

朝鲜特派记者 菲舟

热烈庆祝沪

Celebrating

2019年6月17日 周一 农历己亥年五月十五

大兴机场高速 大兴机场北线高速中段

南五环20多分钟

6月17日 周一 校对 / 刘欣庆 北京晚报

界难题

特

"药性"进程图解

攻坚后

夺能素取合疗法

辅助
配方药 + 夺取药物

眠药后

换

扩大敏感杀虫剂

延长用药

五一七天疗程

11

21 纵闻天下

G20峰会
开幕在即

日本男子袭警

大阪府警称嫌疑人已被逮捕

日本一名男子16日早在大阪府吹田市刺伤一名警察并夺走配枪，枪内有5发子弹。大阪警方发布嫌疑人照片，以涉嫌杀人未遂予以通缉。据日本共同社17日最新消息，大阪府警以抢劫杀人未遂，将33岁的嫌疑人逮捕。报道称，嫌疑人曾持有手枪，其职业不详。

26岁警察身受多处刀伤

16日早晨大约5时40分，警方接到报警，说大阪府吹田市千里山雾之丘的千里山警务站内，一名警官流血倒地。大阪府警方证实，受伤警察是古濑铃之佑，现年26岁，身受多处刀伤，凶器插入他的左胸。

送往医院前，古濑告诉其他警察：

临时中止；在野党立宪民主党党首枝野幸男取消原定16日晚在大阪市的街头演讲。一名49岁女性居民告诉共同记者："希望能在嫌疑人用枪前抓获他。

大阪定于28日、29日召开二十集团（G20）领导人会议。吉村说，如无法在会议举行前把犯罪嫌疑人归案，将与警方商讨对策。

疑有人打假报警电话

【chǐ】

耻【繁体】

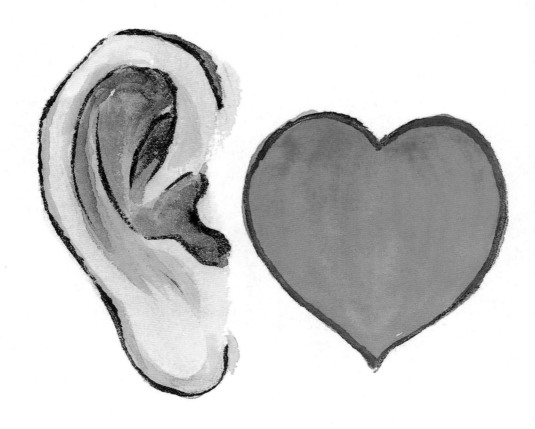

　　"耳"和"心"放在一起，意思是听到别人说自己，说得直心跳、直心慌、真不好意思。这就是"耻"（恥）。

　　This character "耻"（恥）means "shame" or "disgrace". It's a combination of ear "耳" and heart "心" put together. You can think of it as "hearing about something that makes your heart beat quickly".

汉字有意思！2
Hanzi Alive

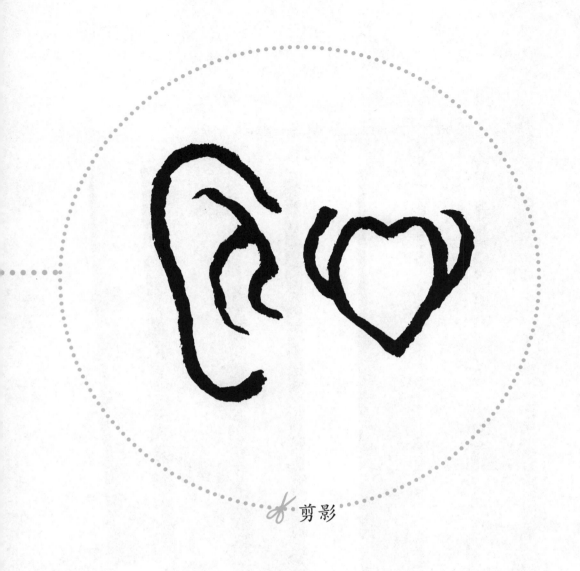

剪影

| 甲骨文 | 金文 | 小篆 | 隶书 | 行书 | 楷体 | 现代简体 |

一起找一找

耻：摄于中国北京。

【shèng】

聖【繁体】

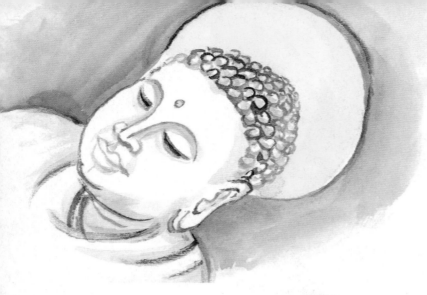

　　人有口，向上天祈祷；上天有耳，听到了，便让植物生长、农作物丰收。这就是"圣"（聖）。

　　中国人尊称道德知识都好的人为"圣人"，又称"圣诞节"为"圣诞"，称孔子为"孔圣"。

People pray to the heavens; God hears their prayers and makes the plants grow, providing a bountiful harvest. This is the symbology behind this character "圣"（聖）, which means "holy". The Chinese honor wise and moral people as "圣人"（holy men）. For example, Confucius（孔子）is also referred to as "孔圣". Christmas is named "圣诞节", literally "holy birth festival".

剪影

甲骨文　金文　小篆　隶书　行书　楷体　现代简体

【niè】

聶【繁体】

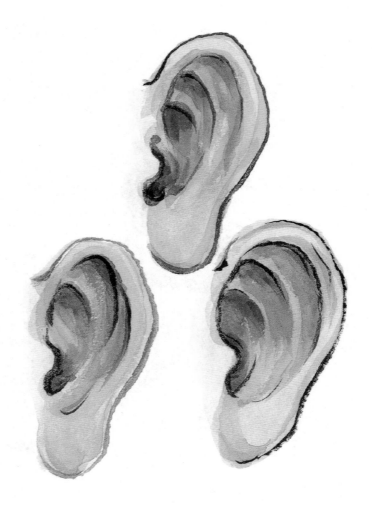

　　三个耳朵摆在一起，好像大家把耳朵凑在一起听悄悄话，这就是形容小声说话的"聂"（聶）。

　　"聂"也是姓。

Three ears together is like three people huddling to hear secrets. This character "聂"（聶）means "to whisper"; it is also a Chinese surname.

剪影

甲骨文	金文	小篆	隶书	行书	楷体	现代简体

一 起 找 一 找

聂：摄于中国北京。

网 吧 ←

北㊙京 稻香村 ←

← 东方园宾馆

聂记麻辣烫

天外天小吃城内 ←

【méi】

眼睛上面一长条，长满毛，是眉毛的"眉"。

A long line drawn above the eye, guess what it can be? The answer is "eyebrow"! This is the character "眉".

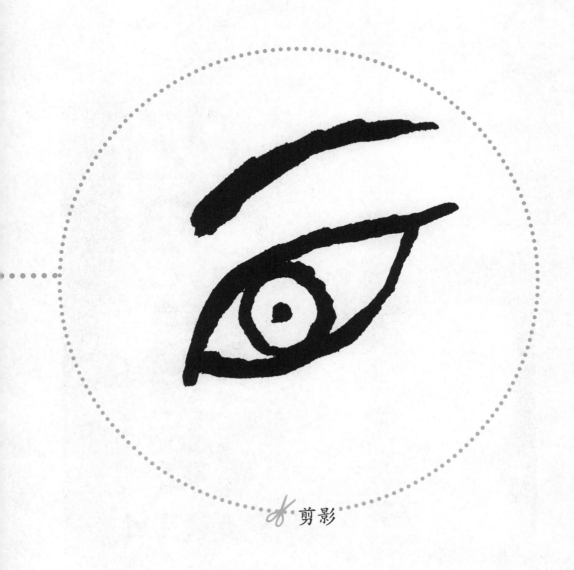

剪影

甲骨文　金文　小篆　隶书　行书　楷体

177

一 起 找 一 找

眉：摄于中国台湾电视台。

眼

【yǎn】

"眼"最早的象形字很传神，就像一个鼻子旁边长着两只眼睛。

The original pictograph for the eye character "眼" looked just like two eyes with a nose in the middle.

剪影

		眼	眼	眼	眼
甲骨文	金文	小篆	隶书	行书	楷体

一起找一找

眼：摄于中国香港。

【 zhòng 】

眾【繁体】

　　上面一只大眼睛，下面三个人，意思是许多人，这个字是"众"（眾）。

　　现在的简体字，把眼睛省略，只写三个人就行了。

A large eye with three persons below it, means "a crowd". This is the character "众"（眾）.

The simplified version of this character did away with the overseeing eye; just three people written together now means "a crowd".

剪影

甲骨文　金文　小篆　隶书　行书　楷体　现代简体

在公众号"新享受"板块中，
点击"我的会员卡"。

新奥购物中心停车优惠开启

点击"停车缴费"。

输入车牌号，
即可完成缴费。

品位文化 自在生活

【shǒu 】

"首"就是"头"，象形字看起来好像一只眼睛上面长了几根毛。

"首" means "the head" or "the beginning". The pictograph looks like an eye with a few hairs on top.

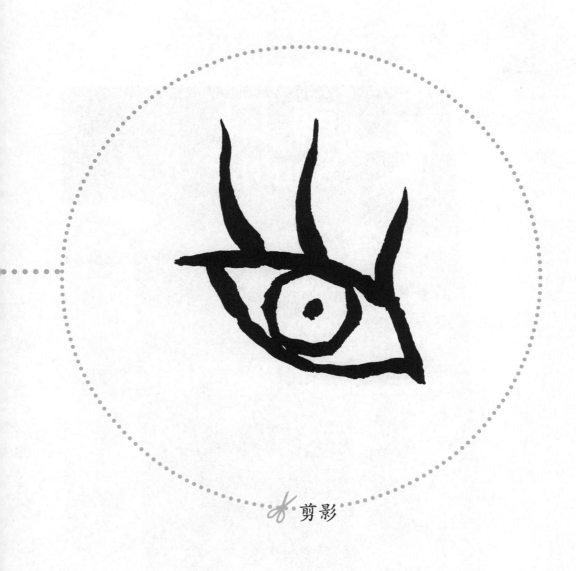

剪影

甲骨文　　金文　　小篆　　隶书　　行书　　楷体

一起找一找
首：摄于日本冲绳。

南口
South Exit

首里城公園
Shurijo Castle Park
首里城公園
슈리조공원

首里金城町石畳道
Shurikinjo Stone Pavement
首里金城町石畳道
슈리킨조초 돌판길

那覇市役所首里支所
Naha City Office : Shuri Branch

首里図書館・公民館
Shuri Library/Community Center

首里鳥堀町 1～5丁目
Shuri Torihoricho 1~5-chome

首里城までは、
徒歩約15～20
分!

南風原町
Haebaru Town

【yè】

頁【繁体】

　　"页"（頁）这个字是由上面一只大眼睛和下面一个人的身体组成的，意思也是头。跟头有关的字，常用"页"做边。譬如"须"，在"页"旁边加三撇，好像三根毛，是胡须的"须"。现今"页"常当作一篇、一张或一面的量词。

　　The character "页"（頁）is made of a large eye on top and a body on the bottom, and it also means "the head". Characters having to do with "the head" often have this "页" as part of it. For example, "须" is "页" with three extra hairs, and means "whiskers".However, "页" is also its own character, meaning "page" （as in the pages of a book）.

剪影

| 甲骨文 | 金文 | 小篆 | 隶书 | 行书 | 楷体 | 现代简体 |

一起找一找

【 sūn 】

孫【繁体】

　　繁体的写法是左边一个"子"，右边一根绳索，表示家族的一代又一代，像绳索一样延伸、牵引下去。这个字是"孙"（孫）。

　　简体写法是"孙"。左边是"子"，右边是"小"，表示比儿子还小一辈的"孙子"。

In this character, there is a "子" on the left, and what appears to be a rope on the right. The rope extends and connects the generations, and thus we have "孙"（孫）, meaning "grandchild".

There is another way to write this character, and that is "孙". In this case, there is a "子" on the left, and a "小"（meaning "small"）on the right. You can think of it as "the child who is smaller than the son".

剪影

甲骨文	金文	小篆	隶书	行书	楷体	现代简体

一起找一找

孙：摄于中国北京。

18　家有一小　　　　　　　　　　　　　　　　　　　　2019年6月17日 周一　　北京晚报

奶奶索要"带孙费"获法院支持

法官表示：她帮带孙女十多年 已超出祖辈正常帮助范畴

■ 故事

从孩子出生第一天 她就帮忙带孙女

■ 起诉

称儿子儿媳不尽责 应付抚养费28万

■ 判决

酌定抚养费10万元 双方均未上诉

■ 法官释法

祖父母没有带孙义务

长期带孙构成无因管理

抚养费用需要综合判断

绘图 王金辉

19

各

德国

【 bǎo 】

　　小娃娃需要保护，由大人守护，所以"保"的左边是"人"，右边是"子"。至于"子"的左右各有一画，应该是后人加上去的。

Babies need the protection of adults, so "保", meaning "protect", is made up of "人"（person）on the left with a "子"（baby）on the right. The two lines on either side of the "baby" appeared later in the character's development.

剪影

甲骨文　金文　小篆　隶书　行书　楷体

一起找一找

保：摄于中国北京故宫。

【zǎi】【zǐ】【zī】

　　"保"如果不加那两笔，就是"仔"，意思是小东西、未成年的孩
子或动物。

　　Without the two extra lines on the baby as in "保", the character becomes
"仔",meaning "little one", referring to small children or baby animals.

剪影

一起找一找

仔：摄于中国台北。

【xì】【jì】

　　"系"最早的写法是用手把几缕丝线连在一起，后来简化成一缕丝线，意思是系统或相互连接的系列。例如，形成长江的河流系统被称为"长江水系"。此外，大学的一个学科是"系"，因为它也指某种系统。例如，中文学科是"中文系"。

　　The earliest form of this character "系" was a hand holding many strands of silk together. Later on, this was simplified into one strand of thread. The meaning of "系" is "a system or interconnecting series". For example, the river system that forms the Yangtze is referred to as "长江水系"（Yangtze water system）. Also, a department of a university is "系", as it also refers to a system of some kind. For example, Chinese department is "中文系".

剪影

甲骨文　金文　小篆　隶书　行书　楷体

【 jué 】

　　绝的意思是"停止"或"切断"。图中象形文字的"绝"，是用一把刀，把成缕的丝线斩断，后来在刀下面加了一个"巴"，成为现在的写法。

　　"绝" means "to stop" or "to cut". The original pictograph shows a knife cutting through strands of woven thread. Later, another part "巴" was added to form today's version of the character.

剪影

| 甲骨文 | 金文 | 小篆 | 隶书 | 行书 | 楷体 | 现代简体 |

一起找一找

绝：摄于中国北京。

【 chuān 】

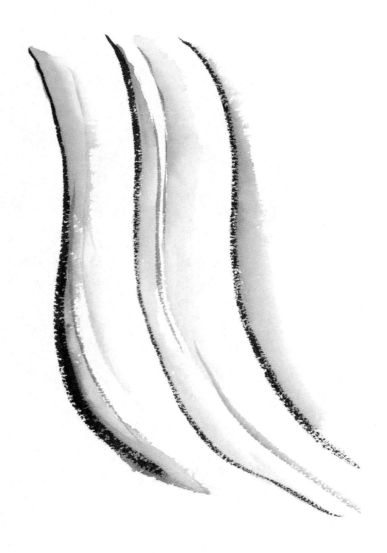

　　"川"字的两边是实线，不像"水"左右各有两条短线，所以川更像一条界线分明的河。在中文里"川"专指河流。

This character was originally very similar to "水", but the two sides of "川" are solid lines with a short dashed line in the middle, resembling the banks of a river with water flowing between them.

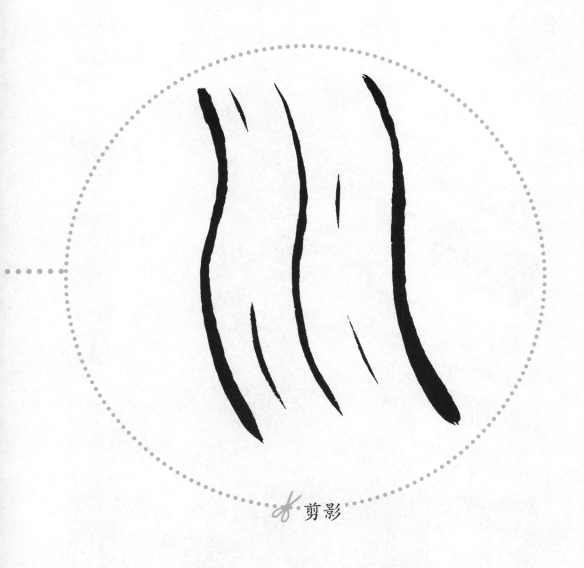

剪影

甲骨文　金文　小篆　隶书　行书　楷体

一起找一找

川：摄于中国台北。

【 zhōu 】

　　在"川"的三条线之间加三个小点，好比河里的小岛，也就是形容"水中地"的"州"字。后来用法扩大了，凡是河与河之间的土地都可以叫"州"。中国人自称中国的领土为"九州"。

Dots between the lines of "川" are like little islands in the river, which is exactly what this character used to describe. Later, the use expanded to mean "any land between rivers". Thus, one of the historical names for mainland China is "九州".

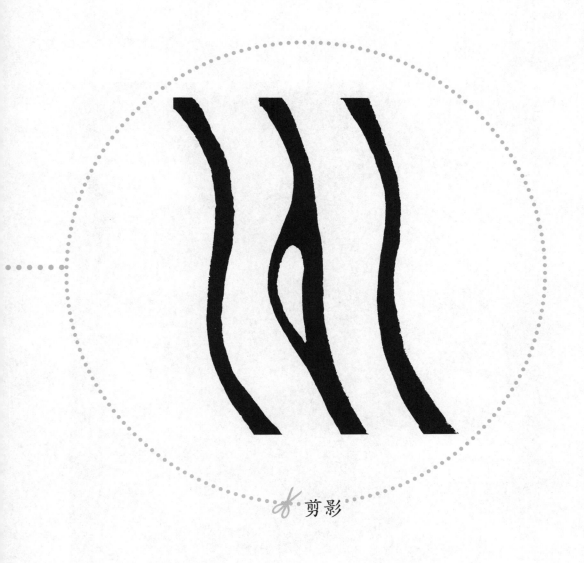

剪影

甲骨文　　金文　　小篆　　隶书　　行书　　楷体

221

【 zhōu 】

　　如果在"州"的左边再加上三个小点，就表示更大的水域之间所夹的土地。譬如亚洲、非洲等，这些大陆，都要用"洲"来形容，而不能用"州"表示。

Adding three extra dots on the left of "州" makes "洲", which refers to land between even larger bodies of water. For example, the continents （such as Asia "亚洲", Africa "非洲" etc.） are all written with this "洲".

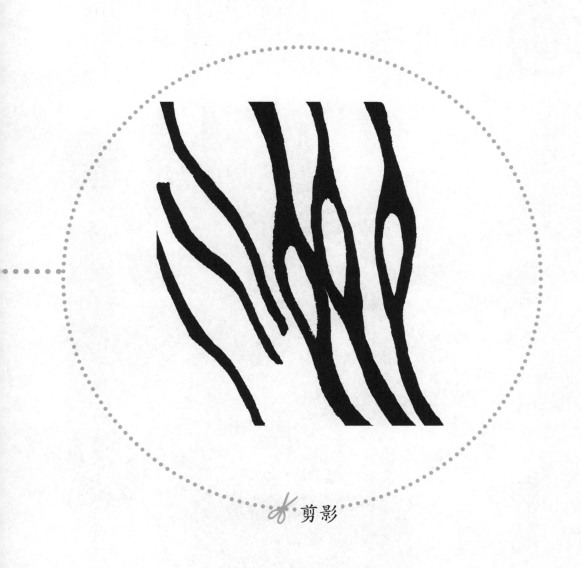

剪影

| | | 甲骨文 | 金文 | 小篆 | 隶书 | 行书 | 楷体 |

225

一起找一找

洲：摄于中国香港。

甲午二○一○年冬　尚草斋　何秀琼　敬献

東方之珠
巨龍邀遊
太平萬世
繁榮九洲

【liú】

　　"流"就像一个人随着河水流动。人头上的三条线，可以表现水流，也可以形容头发。

　　The pictograph of "流" resembles a person floating with a river. The three lines on the person's head can be the flowing water or the person's hair. "流" means "flow", and it can be both a noun and a verb.

剪影

| 甲骨文 | 金文 | 小篆 | 隶书 | 行书 | 楷体 | 现代简体 |

劉墉 与您贴心交流
在生命中
追求爱

【 quán 】

从一个洞里冒出水来，就是"泉"。

Water that comes out of a hole is "a spring", or "泉".

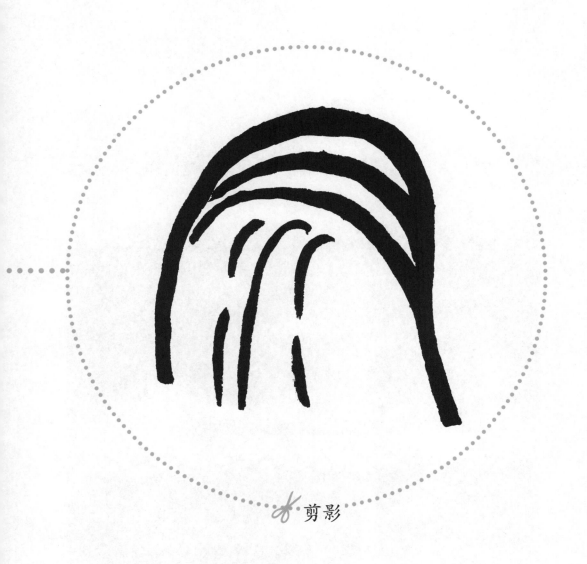

剪影

甲骨文　　金文　　小篆　　隶书　　行书　　楷体

一起找一找

泉：摄于中国山西太原晋祠。

【 yuán 】

　　在象形字"泉"的上面，加弯弯一笔，表示在某样东西下面有泉水。"原"跟"泉"不同，不是明显的，而是隐藏的。所以汉语说"原来"，意思是本来没发现，后来才知晓。

Adding a curved line over the pictograph of "泉" means that the spring is hidden under something. So when the Chinese say "原来", it means "something which was previously unknown, but is apparent now". By itself, "原" means "origin" or "source".

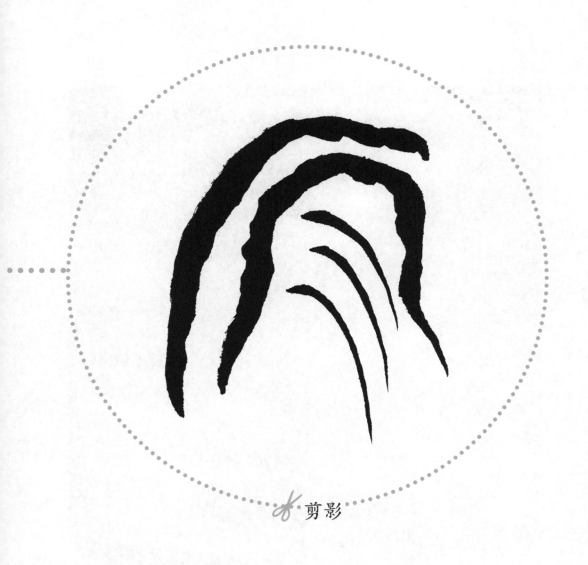

剪影

| 甲骨文 | 金文 | 小篆 | 隶书 | 行书 | 楷体 |

【miáo】

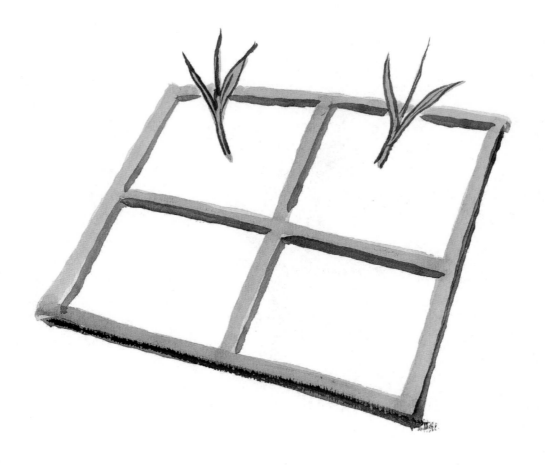

  在田地里长出来的草，是"苗"。苗可以指一切刚萌发的植物，也可以专指人工培育的幼苗。

Grass that grows on farmland is "苗". It can mean "a young plant" "a sprout", or "plants cultivated by people".

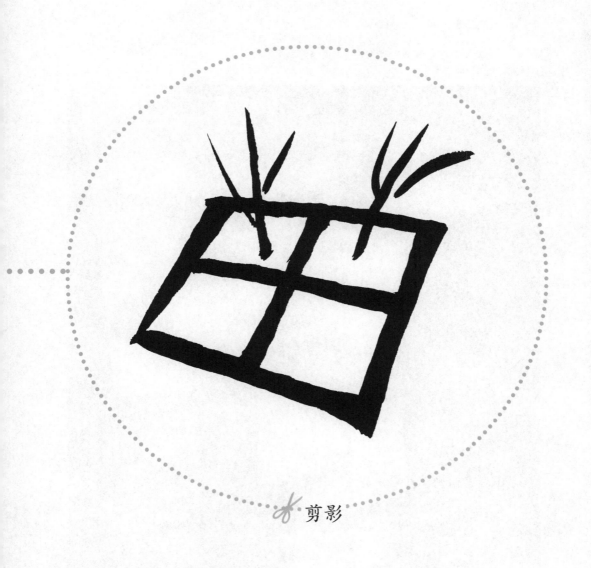

剪影

甲骨文　　金文　　小篆　　隶书　　行书　　楷体　　现代简体

一起找一找

苗：摄于中国台北花市。

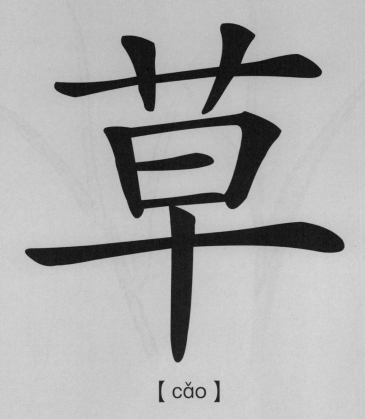

【 cǎo 】

　　"草"是由好像两株小草的象形字演变出来的。汉字中凡是"艹"作部首的,多半跟植物有关。

　　"草" developed from what originally was a pictograph of two clumps of grass. The top part of the character "艹" is used as a radical in the construction of other characters, whose meanings usually have to do with plants.

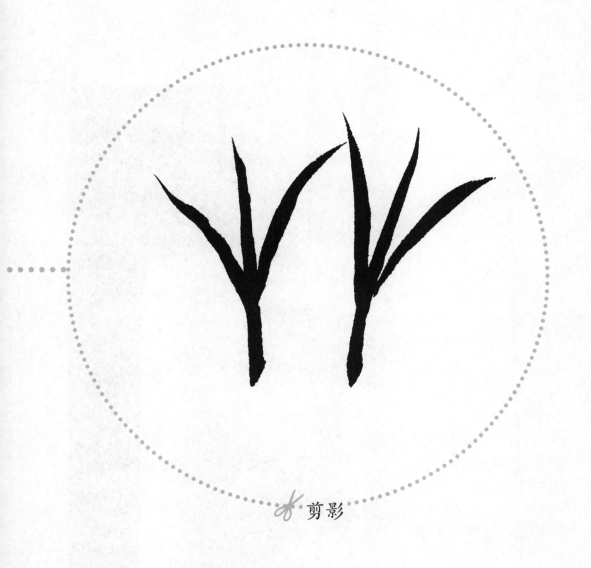

剪影

| 甲骨文 | 金文 | 小篆 | 隶书 | 行书 | 楷体 | 现代简体 |

一起找一找

草：摄于中国北京。

【huì】

　　三株草放在一起，好比把三棵"木"放在一起成为"森"字一样，表示许多草。

Putting three clumps of grass together makes "芔" meaning "lots of grass". It's a similar idea as putting three trees "木" together to make a forest "森".

剪影

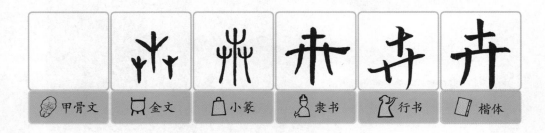

| 甲骨文 | 金文 | 小篆 | 隶书 | 行书 | 楷体 |

一起找一找

卉：摄于中国台北花卉展。

【fèi】

在"犬"左边加一个"口"，成为"吠"，意思是"狗叫"。

This character "吠" is made up of a mouth "口" next to a dog "犬". It means "to bark".

剪影

甲骨文　　金文　　小篆　　隶书　　行书　　楷体

253

一起找一找

吠：摄自《刘墉画集》。

伏

【fú】

　　左边的"人"加上右边的"犬"，不是"人带狗"，而是趴下的意思。好像一只狗乖乖听话趴在地上。当一个人投降、认罪的时候，也称作"伏"。如果趴下不动是为了等敌人不注意的时候起来攻击，称为"埋伏"。

　　You may think that a "人" on the right and a "犬" on the left means "walking the dog", but actually this character "伏" means "to prostrate oneself", much like how a dog lies on the floor. When a person surrenders, it is also called "伏". Prostrating on the ground, ready for a surprise attack on the enemy, would be "埋伏".

剪影

甲骨文	金文	小篆	隶书	行书	楷体

贴

伏

三冬病夏治

减敏·定喘·止咳

【 chòu 】

　　上面画个鼻子，下面画只犬，意思是用鼻子嗅狗，或形容狗的嗅觉很敏锐。又因为狗常常有臭味，所以也形容"臭"。后来为了容易分辨，把用鼻子闻味的"臭"写成"嗅"。"臭"这个字则专形容令人讨厌的气味。

　　A nose above a dog appears to be smelling the dog, or it's describing a dog's sensitive sense of smell. But maybe because dogs can smell bad, this character has come to mean "smelly odor". For clarification, when a mouth "口" is added to "臭", it forms "嗅", which is a verb meaning "to smell", while "臭" is an adjective that means "stinky".

剪影

| 甲骨文 | 金文 | 小篆 | 隶书 | 行书 | 楷体 |

一起找一找

臭：摄于中国台北。

龜苓膏

四季皆宜延年益壽

◆功效◆

養顏美容・清肝降火
煙酒過多・舌乾口臭
通宵熬夜・面皰暗瘡
除濕祛毒・便秘痔瘡

每杯35元

健康食品中之聖品

容家麻糬

【tū】

　　"突"这个字，上面是"穴"，好像一个挂了门帘的山洞。从山洞里猝不及防地跳出一只狗，就是"突然"的"突"。

　　"突" means "suddenly". The "穴" on top looks like the entrance to a cave. If you imagine a dog suddenly jumping out of a cave, it′s not difficult to understand the origin of this word.

剪影

甲骨文　　金文　　小篆　　隶书　　行书　　楷体

265

【rán】

　　既然学了突然的"突"，也就介绍一下"然"这个字。

　　"然"也跟狗有关，但它是三个象形字合在一起。左上方是"月"（前面讲过那像一块肉），右上方是"犬"，下面是"火"，意思是烤狗肉。所以"然"最早的意思是"烧"，但是后来变成"这样子"的意思。要形容燃烧的时候，则在左边再加个"火"字，成为"燃"。

　　"然" is made up of three pictographs. In the upper left is "月", which in this case means "meat". In the upper right is "犬"（dog）, and on the bottom is "灬" for "fire". All together, it means "to cook（dog）meat". "然" used to mean "to burn", but since then the meaning has departed from its original use; today, "然" means "so", as in "it is so". Another "火"（fire）was added to the original "然" to mean "to burn", and it is also pronounced as "rán".

剪影

| 甲骨文 | 金文 | 小篆 | 隶书 | 行书 | 楷体 |

應坐以人事順坐

以天理行坐以丑

德應坐以自然

【 chóng 】

　　"虫"是象形字，最早像是蝌蚪或蛇的样子，渐渐变成"虫"。后来为了表示虫很多，也把"虫"写成"蟲"，像是三只虫在一起。

　　"虫" is the pictograph meaning "insect". You can see the evolution of the character from being tadpole-like to become today's "虫". Later, the Chinese started also writing "蟲" as "虫", which puts three bugs together to depict a multitude of insects.

剪影

| 甲骨文 | 金文 | 小篆 | 隶书 | 行书 | 楷体 | 现代简体 |

一起找一找

虫：摄于中国北京。

【mǎng】

　　一只狗在草丛里跑，形容一片大的野草地。"莽原"是大草原，"莽蛇"是大蛇。

A dog is running in a large grassy field. "莽" generally means "grass". "莽原" is a meadow, while "莽蛇" is a large snake that presumably dwells in the grass.

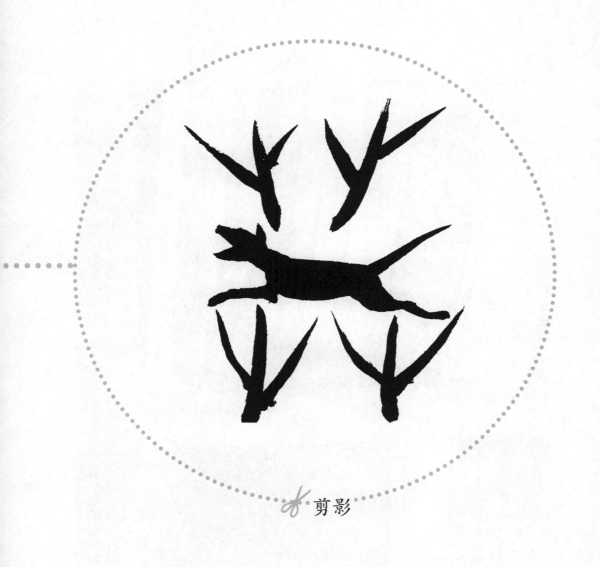

剪影

甲骨文　金文　小篆　隶书　行书　楷体　现代简体

一起找一找

莽：摄于中国台北。

【 shé 】

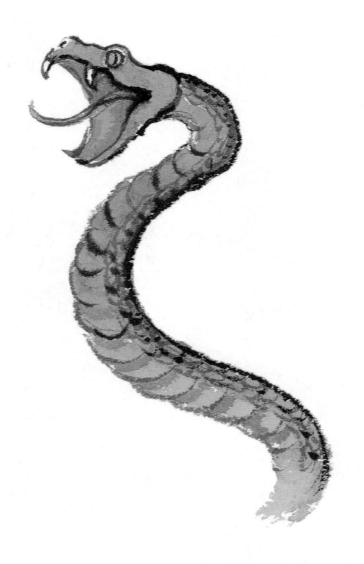

　　"蛇"的象形字就像一只响尾蛇的头。后来汉字又为它分类，表示它是一种"虫"，所以在"它"的左边加了一个"虫"。

　　"蛇" means "snake". The original pictograph resembles the head of a cobra. Later on, the Chinese classified snakes together with insects, and thus placed a "虫" radical next to "它".

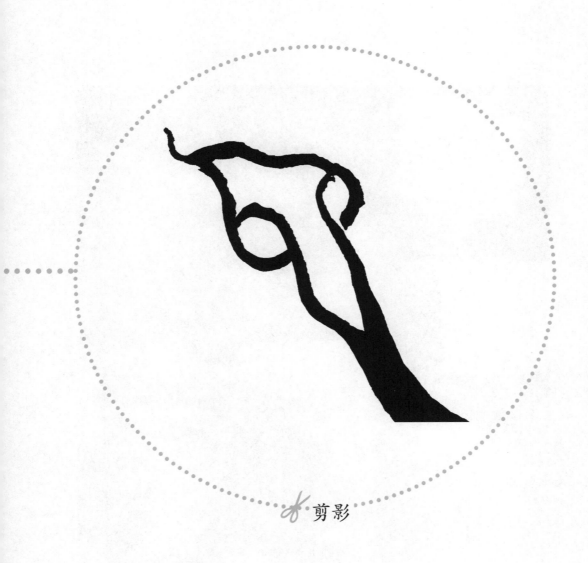

剪影

| 甲骨文 | 金文 | 小篆 | 隶书 | 行书 | 楷体 |

一起找一找

蛇:摄于中国台北花市。

【zǎo】

跳蚤咬人，好痒啊，快用手抓痒！

这个字上面是手，手之间好像有小虫，下面又有只大虫，表现了人在抓跳蚤。

Fleas make people very itchy, itchy and scratchy! "蚤" means "flea".

The top part of this character is a hand with what looks like little bugs between the fingers, and below is a larger bug, to make the point even clearer.

剪影

| 甲骨文 | 金文 | 小篆 | 隶书 | 行书 | 楷体 | 现代简体 |

一起找一找

蚤：摄于中国台北。

蚓

【yǐn】

　　"蚓"是蚯蚓，可以说它有三部分，最左边是虫，中间是一条弯曲的长虫，右边是一条直直的长虫，加在一起就成了那种能弯曲又能伸直的虫。

"蚓" is part of the term "蚯蚓", which means "earthworm".

"蚓" is made of three parts: an insect radical（虫）on the left, a wiggly worm in the middle, and a straight long worm on the right. Together, they depict an insect that can both bend and straighten, ie. an earthworm!

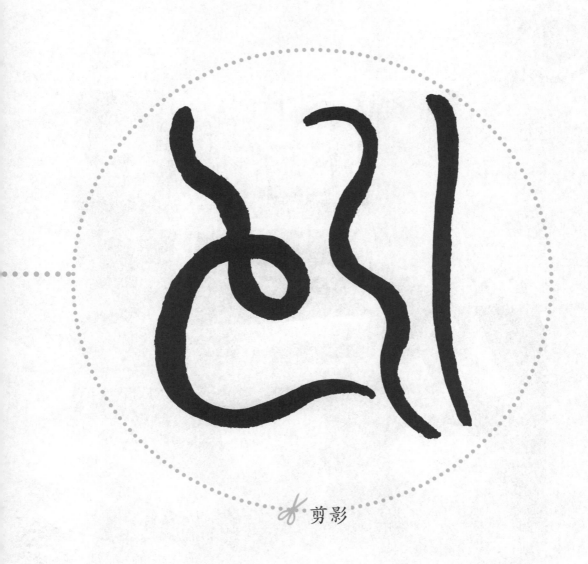

剪影

一起找一找

蚓：摄于中国台北花市。

【wū】

鸟 【繁体】

　　"鸟"这个字如果少了眼睛就是"乌"字。乌指乌鸦,是黑色的鸟,它的瞳孔也是黑色的,远看跟身体的黑混在一起,好像没了眼睛,所以写成"乌"。乌也用来指一切黑的东西,如"乌云""乌发"。

　　A bird "鸟" that is missing an eye is "乌", which is a crow. Crows are black, and since their eyes are also black, they appear eyeless from far away. "乌" can also be used in terms describing anything black, such as "乌云"（dark cloud）and "乌发"（black hair）.

剪影

| 甲骨文 | 金文 | 小篆 | 隶书 | 行书 | 楷体 | 现代简体 |

【 què 】

　　上面写个"小"字，下面写个"隹"，意思是小鸟。因为平常见的小鸟多半是麻雀，所以后来专指麻雀这类小鸟。

　　A "小"（small）on top and a "隹" on the bottom form a character that means "little bird". Since sparrows are some of the most common little birds we see, "雀" has now come to mean "sparrow" specifically.

剪影

甲骨文　金文　小篆　隶书　行书　楷体

【 jiāo 】

　　在火上烤鸟，火一大就烤焦了，这个字是"焦"。"焦"除了可以形容烤焦的东西，也可以形容紧急的状况，好比一个人发现鸡被烤焦了而手忙脚乱的焦急样子。

When you roast a bird over a fire, it is very easy to overcook it. Thus we have "焦" as the word for "burnt".

"焦" can also be used to describe a state of anxiety, presumably such as when someone finds out that their chicken has been burnt!

剪影

甲骨文　　金文　　小篆　　隶书　　行书　　楷体

一起找一找

焦：摄于中国台北 Starbucks。

	中杯 Tall	大杯 Grande
	105	120
	105	120
	90	105
	90	105
	105	120
	80	95

❄

	Solo	Doppio
	50	65
	60	75
	60	75

Starbucks On Ice
沁涼系列

		中杯 Tall	大杯 Grande
冰焦糖瑪奇朵 *Iced Caramel Macchiato*		105	120
冰那堤 *Iced Caffé Latte*		90	105
冰摩卡 *Iced Caffé Mocha*		105	120
冰美式咖啡 *Iced Caffé Americano*		80	95
冰搖雙份濃縮咖啡 *Starbucks DoubleShot Iced Shaken Espresso* （咖啡/焦糖/香草 *Coffee/ Caramel/ Vanilla*）	95(7oz)		
冰泰舒茶 *Iced Tazo Tea*		80	90
100%柳橙汁 *100% Orange Juice*		80	
100%有機蘋果汁 *100% Organic Apple Juice*		90	

＊自備咖啡杯可享10元折扣

【qú】

一只睁着两个大眼睛的鸟是"瞿",形容老鹰的眼神。

人看到大老鹰,会被吓一跳,所以"瞿"也形容人受惊害怕的样子。如果再加个"心"字旁,就是惧怕的"惧"。

A bird with two very large eyes is "瞿", which describes an eagle's expression. When people see eagles, they also get frightened, so "瞿" also came to describe how people look when they are scared. If you add a "心"（heart）radical to the character, it would form "惧", pronounced the same way and used in "惧怕", which means "frightened".

剪影

		瞿	瞿	瞿	瞿
甲骨文	金文	小篆	隶书	行书	楷体

一起找一找

瞿：摄于中国台北。

【jiù】

舊【繁体】

　　"旧"（舊）字太有意思了！看起来像一只带着长长耳羽的鸟，站在鸟窝上，最早的意思是猫头鹰。古人常看到猫头鹰到别的小鸟窝里，抢人家的蛋、吃人家的雏鸟，于是用这个"旧"字来形容。但后来不知为什么，变成了形容老的、过时的东西，不再用来指猫头鹰了。

　　This character has a curious past. A bird with long ears standing in a nest—that is the drawing of an owl. People long ago often saw owls invading other birds' nests and stealing their eggs for food. That is how "旧" came to be. But for reasons unclear to us, "旧" is now the word for "old" and "worn out", and no longer is related to the owls.

剪影

| 甲骨文 | 金文 | 小篆 | 隶书 | 行书 | 楷体 | 现代简体 |

一起找一找

旧：摄于中国北京。

【jù】

　　下面三个人，上面一只手正捂着耳朵说悄悄话，这就是"聚"，意思是许多人在一起。想想那三个人"咬耳朵"，说张家长、李家短的样子，这个字多生动啊！

Three people on the bottom and a hand shielding an ear （for a whisper） combine to form "聚", meaning "to gather". It's not hard to vividly imagine this as a picture of three people gossiping.

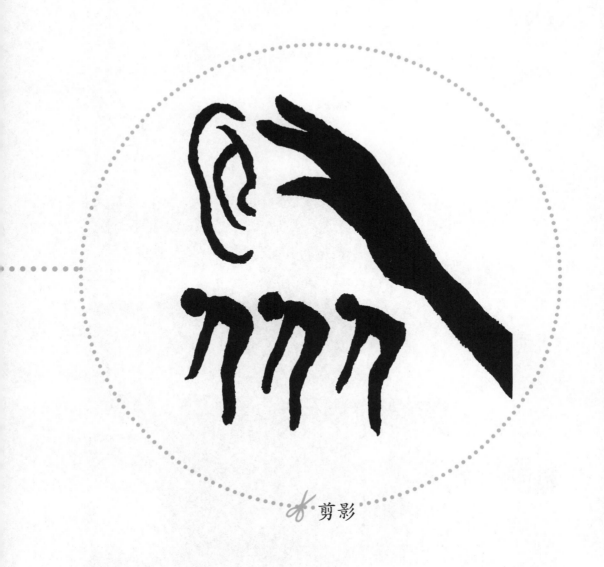

剪影

| 甲骨文 | 金文 | 小篆 | 隶书 | 行书 | 楷体 | 现代简体 |

313

一起找一找

聚：摄于中国香港。

慇慇乎厱佛
救溺扶危好
財来自有方
德聚福無量
行善壽而康

方德福 方正文 方正安 敬獻

一九九一年夏月

【chū】

　　盆里种了种子，钻出土壤发芽了，这就是"出"。后来渐渐演变成两个"山"叠在一起，好像"山"上有"山"。

　　到中国旅行，一定要知道这个字，通常公共场所会加个"口"，写成"出口"，意思是那边有个可以出去的口。

Seeds in a pot have sprouted from the soil. This is "出", meaning "out" or "exit". The character now looks like two mountains on top of each other.

This is another word that you must know when visiting China. Public places usually have signs that say "出口", which means "exit".

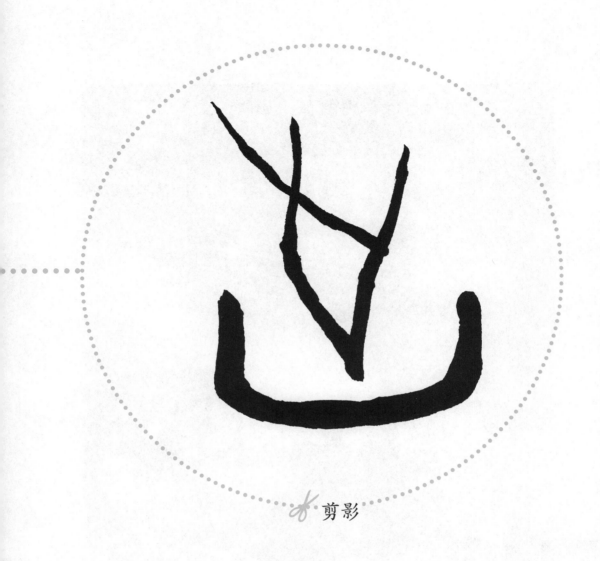

剪影

甲骨文　金文　小篆　隶书　行书　楷体

317

一起找一找

出：摄于日本冲绳。

【rù】

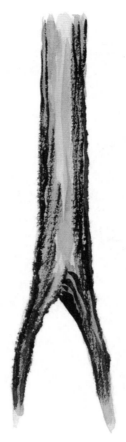

　　懂得"出"，就得认得"入"。出是冒出土，发芽了。入则像植物扎根进入土壤。跟出口相似，中国人常在"入"字后面加个"口"，即"入口"，意思是你可以从那里进去。你或许会问为什么先教"出"，才教"入"，这是因为到了紧要关头，能够让你逃生的"出口"更重要。

If you understand "出", then you must also learn "入". "出" is a sprout exiting soil, and "入" looks like a plant's roots growing in the soil. Chinese add "口" next to "入", and "入口" means "entrance". You may wonder why we choose to teach you "exit" before "entrance", and the reason is that we think it's much more important to know the signs for "出口" in an emergency situation!

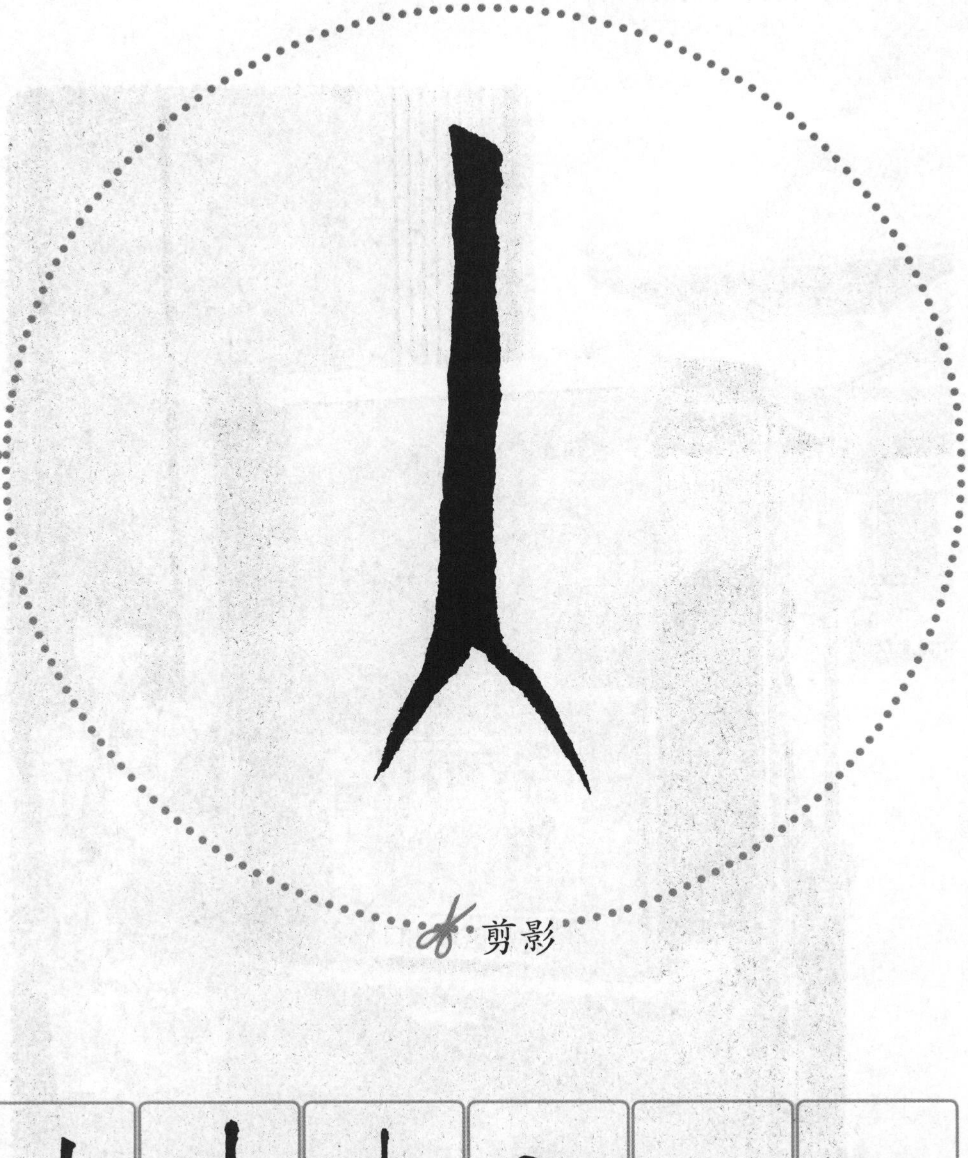

剪影

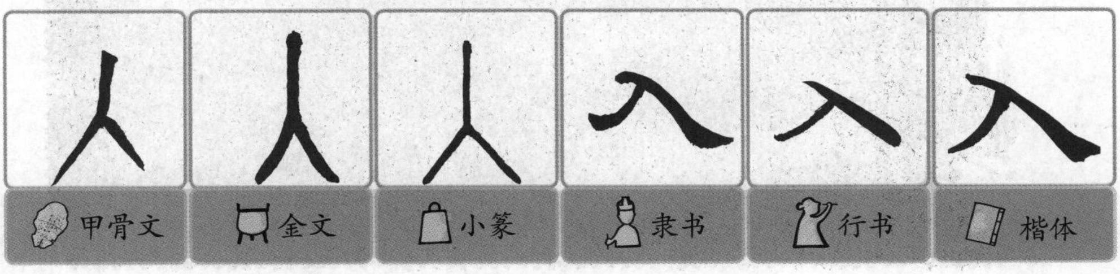
甲骨文
金文
小篆
隶书
行书
楷体

一起找一找

入：摄于日本冲绳首里城。

汉字是怎么演进的
The evolution of Hanzi Characters

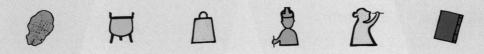

甲骨文

中国人的老祖先很迷信，碰上重要的事，像能不能打仗、什么时候适合种田打猎、什么时候会下雨，甚至王后会生男孩还是女孩，都要问老天爷。

他们问的方法很特殊——先在乌龟肚皮上的那块甲壳或其他野兽的骨头上钻个小孔，再把一小块烧红的炭或金属放在那小洞上，甲骨被烤焦而且膨胀造成裂纹，那些巫师则根据裂纹的样子解说老天爷给的答案，再把答案刻在裂纹的旁边。

这些由公元前一千多年留存到今天的甲骨文上的文字，可以说是中国最早的文字。

由于甲骨文是用金属刀子刻在很硬的甲骨上，所以多半线条很细、笔触很直、头尾比较尖。又因为当时的文字还没统一，所以同一个字可能刻得不同，而且许多像图画，比较容易猜出它的意思。

我们由这些最早的甲骨文开始，一点一点看它们后来的演变，就好像先找到山里的小溪，再顺着溪水往下，很容易就能找到大河一样，也就能很轻松地学会现在的汉字了。

书里凡是作"  "这个好像"乌龟肚皮甲"符号的都是甲骨文。

商晚期·甲骨文
Oracle bone with inscriptions,late Shang Dynasty.

Oracle Bone and Tortoise Shell Inscriptions
Shang Dynasty (c.16th 11th century B.C.)

The ancient people of China were very superstitious. When faced with any important issue, such as whether or not the country should go to war, when it would be most suitable to farm or to hunt, how long it would be until the next rainfall, or even whether the queen would give birth to a boy or a girl, the Chinese consulted the gods.

Their method of divination involved first puncturing the interior side of tortoise shells or the bones of other animals. When a small piece of red—hot coal or metal was placed over the holes, the burnt shells or bones expanded, resulting in cracks. The oracle then interpreted the cracks as heaven's response and carved the explanation next to the cracks.

Such oracle inscriptions were produced with metal blades on hard surfaces, most of the strokes were extremely fine and straight with pointed ends. Without a unified writing system, one word could have been carved in many different ways, most of which looked like pictures.

We begin from these ancient oracle inscriptions to see how characters gradually evolved. Just like finding a small mountain stream, following its path, and coming upon a great river, we will easily learn and understand modern—day Chinese characters.

In this book, oracle inscriptions will be indicated by " " (tortoise shell symbol).

金 文

　　既然刻甲骨文是用刀，表示中国人早已使用金属工具。考古学家也确实挖掘到不少当时以金属（主要是青铜）制造的武器和餐具。其中的餐具尤其讲究，像是煮食物的"鼎"、盛东西的"盘"、装酒的"壶"，上面不但有美丽的花纹，而且常常刻铸了文字。起初那文字很简单，可能只像个商标图案，渐渐越刻越多，甚至成为整篇大文章。

　　在铜器上刻字或铸字，比在甲骨上麻烦得多，也自然要小心得多。所以铜器上留下来的字，多半比较整齐、笔触较粗、分布得较平均，也修饰得比较美。而且因为不用甲骨占卜之后，中国人还不断制造青铜器，所以上面的金文呈现了许多比甲骨文晚的字。

　　书中凡是作"鼎"状"㫑"符号的，都是金文。

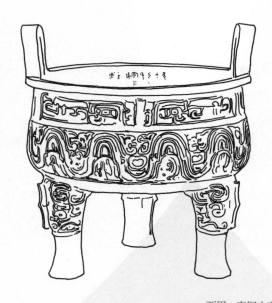

西周·青铜小克鼎
Bronze xiaoke Ding, Western Zhou.

Bronzeware Inscriptions

The production of oracle inscriptions by a sharp knife reveals that the Chinese had already started using metal tools. Archaeologists excavated numerous metal, especially bronze, weapons and cooking utensils. The utensils were particularly intricate; there were three-legged cooking vessels, plates, and wine bottles with beautiful embellishments and often even inscriptions. At first, those characters were simply symbols; the words gradually increased and became sentences and paragraphs.

Inscribing on bronze is much more difficult than carving into bones or tortoise shells, and requires more precision. Therefore, bronzeware inscriptions are usually neater and laid out more evenly with thicker strokes and more elaborate ornaments. While the practice of bone and tortoise shell divination came to an end, the Chinese people continued to produce bronzeware. Because of this, bronzeware inscriptions display Chinese characters of a later period than oracle inscriptions.

西周·青铜小克鼎铭文
Inscriptions on bronze Xiaoke Ding, Western Zhou.

小 篆

公元前二二一年，秦始皇统一中国，他除了统一全国度量衡和车轮的距离，而且命令宰相李斯把原先写法不同的文字标准化，是为"小篆"，至于未统一之前的文字则称为"大篆"。两百年后，东汉的许慎又写了一本《说文解字》，对小篆的源流做了分析。

在这本书里凡标注秤砣符号"⚖"的都是根据《说文解字》写的"小篆"，对比之前的大篆，每个字都成为更整齐的方块字，笔触也更均匀，汉字到了这个时候已经称得上相当进步。

清·邓石如·篆书册
Small Seal Script,by Deng Shiru,Qing Dynasty.

Small Seal Script

In 221 B.C., China came under the rule of its first emperor, Qin Shi Huang. In order to unify his empire, he developed a network of roads and standardized the axles of carts. Most importantly, he ordered Prime Minister Li Si to systematize Qin script by removing its variant forms, thereby creating an official set of Chinese characters, which was later called small seal script. Writing from before the standardization is known as large seal script.

After 200 years, Xu Shen of the Eastern Han Dynasty wrote *Shuowen Jiezi*, a dictionary which analyzed the origin and meaning of every small seal script character.

In this book, I use the symbol of a weight " 🔔 " to signify all excerpts from *Shuowen Jiezi*. One can see that small seal script is more orderly than oracle inscriptions and bronzeware inscriptions. Most of the words appear rectangular with more uniform brush strokes; these are already very advanced Chinese characters.

竹木简牍书

研究中国文字，不能不了解中国人的毛笔。因为必须有很好用的毛笔，中国书法才能发展得那么变化多端。

从史前陶器上的花纹和甲骨上写的字，可以知道那时候已经有了不错的毛笔。甲骨文不是刻的吗，为什么还有毛笔写的痕迹呢？那是因为当时的人常先用黑墨或朱红色的颜料写一遍，然后再刻。有些字写好了没刻，所以现在能看到。

由铜器上的文字笔触，也可以看出古人多半先用毛笔写好、用刀刻好再铸。可惜既然做成铜器，就再也看不到原来的笔迹了。

现在的人，如果想看中国人老祖先的笔迹，最好的材料是公元前五世纪左右留下的写在木简和竹简上的文字。而且因为那些字都只需写，不必刻，有些只是账册、书信甚至日记，所以写得特别自由，由此可以看出很多潇洒而有个性的表现，逐渐把中国文字从拘谨的篆体中解放出来。

当时，中国人把一根根长长的竹片或木片用绳子编在一起。中文一直用到今天的"册"字，就是"两条竹木简中间穿一根绳子"的"象形字"。传说孔子"读《易》，韦编三绝"，也表示孔子当时读的是用皮绳子编的竹简或木简。

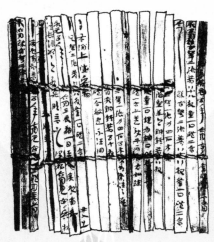

居延汉简
Writing slips, Han Dynasty.

Wood and Bamboo Slip Inscriptions

To truly know Chinese characters, one must understand the Chinese brush. Chinese calligraphy could only develop so much variation with such a writing utensil.

Designs on ancient pottery and oracle inscriptions on bones are evidence of an already quite advanced brush at that time. You may be wondering, were' t oracle inscriptions carved? Then why are there still traces of a brush? That is because people often first used black ink or red pigment to write the characters as a guide for engraving. Some words were written but not carved and thus can now be seen.

From the brush stokes apparent in characters on bronze, one can see that they were usually first written with a brush and then carved. However, only bronze objects, and not their molds, have been preserved; we will never be able to actually see the original writing technique.

If people today wish to observe the handwriting of their ancestors, the best subjects would be the characters written on wood, bamboo slips, and silk （c. 5th century B.C.）. Because they were only written and not engraved, they were composed freely, often in the form of account books, letters, and diaries. They were natural and individualistic expressions that helped to release Chinese language from the rigid seal script.

The Chinese word "册", which still means "volume（of a book）", is a pictograph of a string going through the middle of two bamboo slips.

There is a story about Confucius reading *The Book of Changes* so much that the leather straps broke three times, which also implies that he studied from volumes of wood and bamboo slips.

隶 书

　　教育越来越进步、知识越来越丰富、书信越来越普遍，加上公元前一世纪左右有了纸的发明，中国人觉得篆字实在太不方便了，因为既要在转弯的地方画得圆，又得把线条写得匀，非常费时间。于是开始改变，笔触向两边伸长，这样摆动的"隶书"就出现了。如果形容写篆字是把双手绑起来跳舞，"隶书"则是松了绑，你可以很容易地看出写字的人自由多了——本来圆形的框子现在成为方形，尤其向左右的"撇"和"捺"，先压一下，再挑起来，十分潇洒。

　　中文"隶书"的"隶"，意思是"在下面乖乖听话做事的人"，也可以解释为底层公务员，因为隶书是下面办事人员图方便和快速最先使用的字体。为了书写方便，中国文字由巫师使用的"甲骨文"、贵族使用的"金文"，秦始皇统一的"小篆"到汉代的"隶书"，真是越来越实用而且平民化了。

　　书里凡是作"  "这种"文书人员写字"图案的都是隶书。

汉·史晨前后碑
Shi Chen Bei,Han Dynasty.

Clerical Script

With improving education, increasing knowledge, wide use of written messages and the invention of paper around 1st century B.C., the Chinese people were starting to feel the inconvenience of small seal script, which was extremely time consuming to write because of its rounded edges and identical strokes. The extended and flexible brush strokes of clerical script therefore developed. Writing clerical script is like dancing with hands unbound. The formerly round frame is now rectangular; the ends of strokes involve slightly pressing down and then raising the brush, all in a carefree manner.

Because this script made record keeping quick and easy, and was used by government clerics, it is thus known as "clerical script". As we can see, the evolution of characters has moved towards convenience and accessibility. Originally only used by oracles, then by royals (bronzeware inscription), then standardized (small seal script), and used widely by clerics in the Han Dynasty, writing became more practical and familiar to daily life.

In this book, I will use " " (office worker) to symbolize clerical script.

行书·草书

如果说"篆书"是坐、"隶书"是走，"行书"应该是跑，"草书"则是飞。

虽然"隶书"写起来已比"篆书"快，为了实用，人们还是不满意，他们要写得更快，于是有了"行书"和"草书"。我们很难说行书和草书产生于什么时候，因为就算早在公元前三世纪还是以小篆为主的秦代，如果打仗时军情紧急，为了求快，也会写行书和草书。但是至少可以说，到四世纪的王羲之、王献之父子，行书和草书已经发展到巅峰。

行书和草书最大的特色是它们转动得比隶书圆滑。为了求快，写字的人不再费时间慢慢表现每笔的开头和收尾，而是上一笔连着下一笔写，就算不是真的相连，每笔之间也好像有一根无形的线牵着。"行书"比"隶书"写得快，但比"飞快"的"草书"还慢些。所以行书笔触连得少，不像草书有时候好几个字不但笔笔相连，而且字字相连，好像拉起其中一根线，所有的字都能被扯起来。

因为中国文人特别爱写行书，以前又流行在墙壁上题诗，所以书中凡是有"文人在墙上题字"" "符号的，都是行书或草书。

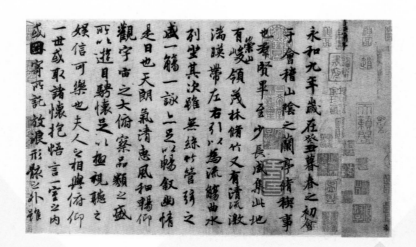

晋·王羲之·兰亭集序（神龙本）
Lantingji Xu, by Wang Xizhi, Jin Dynasty.

Semi–cursive and Cursive Script

If characters had movement, then seal script would be like sitting; clerical script would be like walking, semi–cursive script would be like running, and cursive script would be like flying!

Although clerical script was already much more convenient than small seal script, people wanted to write faster, and developed semi–cursive and cursive script. It is hard to say exactly when these scripts were created because even when small seal script was officially used during the Qin Dynasty, military messages required such speed that they were often written in semi–cursive and cursive script. At the very least, one can say that both these scripts were developed to their fullest extent by the 4th century, as evident in the calligraphy of father and son Wang Xizhi and Wang Xianzhi.

The greatest characteristic of semi–cursive and cursive script is the smooth motion. Writers no longer stop at the beginning and end of every stroke. Instead, each stroke follows the previous; even if they do not actually connect, they seem to be attached by an invisible line. This is especially apparent in cursive script, where not only strokes but often even multiple characters are joined, as if pulling the end of one line would raise the entire sentence off the page.

Because Chinese scholars preferred to use semi–cursive script and also because writing poems on walls used to be popular, " " will signify semi–cursive or cursive script in the book.

楷书

楷书又叫"真书"或"正书"，是从七世纪初，中国就一直使用至今的标准字体。1949 年后，中国大陆又简化了其中一些字，称为"简体字"。而香港、台湾地区还在使用未经简化的"楷书"，称为"正体字"或"繁体字"。

楷书应该是与行书、草书同时发展出来的，也可以说为了写得快，并且使上一笔与下一笔更容易连接，楷书是在隶书的基础上，加了行书和草书的一些笔触。例如，小篆的"手"字边是"🖐"，隶书的"手"字边是"扌"，草书的"手"字边写成"扌"，楷书的"手"字边则成为"扌"。

比起较死板的小篆和沉重的隶书，楷书增加了许多轻巧、像小鸟啄食的"点"和"钩""提"，这些笔触因为都是"重重落笔、轻轻出笔"，一头钝、一头尖，所以写起来快些，看起来也轻巧些。虽不像草书可以好几笔相连那么快，但是比起篆、隶，它是既工整又比较好写的字体。自七世纪以来，中国人凡是重要的公文绝大多数使用楷书。

这本书里凡作"线装书"符号"▱"的，都是楷书。

唐·柳公权·大达法师玄秘塔碑
Xuan Mi Ta Bei, by Liu Gongquan, Tang Dynasty.

Regular Script

Regular script, also known as true script and standard script, is the Chinese calligraphy style that has been used from the early 7th century to modern times. After 1949, the mainland China simplified some characters, however, Taiwan and Hong Kong still use Regular Script, which is now called Traditional Chinese.

Regular script developed during approximately the same time as semi‑cursive and cursive script. To write faster with better connected strokes, regular script has some cursive characteristics and the basis of clerical script. For example, the radical that means hand is "φ" in small seal script, "才" in clerical script, "扌" in cursive script, and "扌" in regular script.

Compared to the rigid small seal script and the heavy clerical script, regular script has many light dots, hooks, and lifts. The style is the result of landing the brush solidly and raising it gently, giving each stroke one dull end and one sharp end. Although it is not as fast to write as cursive script, it is certainly neat and efficient. Since the 7th century, the Chinese have used regular script for most official documents.

In the book, " [] " will symbolize regular script.

简体汉字

严格说，一般所称的"中文字"，应该叫作"汉字"，因为中国许多民族也有自己的文字，只因汉人占大多数，所以采取汉字为全国通用的文字。

今天的简体汉字，除了少数是新造的，许多都在以前的行书或草书中出现过。也可以说，虽然从七世纪到二十一世纪，中国人都用"楷书"，但是人们为了求快，早就发展出一些简体字。譬如"幾"写成"几"、"畫"写成"画"、"舉"写成"举"、"舊"写成"旧"、"龜"写成"龟"、"勸"写成"劝"、"區"写成"区"、"慶"写成"庆"、"親"写成"亲"、"橋"写成"桥"、"豈"写成"岂"、"盡"写成"尽"、"擊"写成"击"、"還"写成"还"、"蝦"写成"虾"、"開"写成"开"、"會"写成"会"、"國"写成"国"、"龍"写成"龙"、"劉"写成"刘"、"麗"写成"丽"、"歷"写成"历"、"難"写成"难"、"頭"写成"头"、"廳"写成"厅"、"達"写成"达"、"當"写成"当"、"豐"写成"丰"、"無"写成"无"、"寶"写成"宝"。以上这些字，就算完全不懂中文的人也可以看得出"后者"好写得多。

此外，中国大陆也根据行书和草书简化了"偏旁"。譬如"言"字旁写成"讠"，"食"字旁写成"饣"，"车"字边写成"车"。由此可知，学习四世纪的行书和草书，对认识今天的"简体汉字"也有帮助。汉字再怎么变，都是血脉相通的。

Simplified Chinese

Technically, what we now call "Chinese characters" should be called "Han characters". The numerous tribes of ancient China all had their own language; because Han had the largest population, Han characters were chosen to be China's official writing system.

Except for those that were newly created, the majority of modern simplified Chinese characters had appeared in semi-cursive or cursive script. Even though regular script was used from the 7th to the 21st century, people developed some simplified characters for speed. Examples are shown in the table below. Obviously, the simplified characters are easier to write.

Much of this simplification is actually based on semi-cursive and cursive script. For example, "言" (speech) is written as "讠", "食" (food) as "饣", "车" (car) as "车". Learning about the semi-cursive and cursive script of the 4th century can thus help us to better appreciate modern-day simplified Chinese. Regardless of how much Chinese characters change, they are all still related by lineage.

楷书 Regular Script	幾	畫	舉	舊	龜	勸	區	慶	親	橋
简体汉字 Simplified Chinese	几	画	举	旧	龟	劝	区	庆	亲	桥

楷书 Regular Script	豈	盡	擊	還	蝦	開	會	國	龍	劉
简体汉字 Simplified Chinese	岂	尽	击	还	虾	开	会	国	龙	刘

楷书 Regular Script	麗	難	頭	廳	達	當	豐	無	寶
简体汉字 Simplified Chinese	丽	难	头	厅	达	当	丰	无	宝

◆ 作者简介
About the Authors

刘墉 Yung Liu

闻名海峡两岸的画家、作家、教育家。出版文学艺术作品一百余种，被译为英、韩、泰、越等国文字，在世界各地举办绘画个展三十余次。

One of the most influential and popular writers of the Chinese speaking world, and also a renowned painter and educator, Mr. Liu has written over one hundred books of essays, prose, short fiction, inspiration literature and art analysis, and his books have been translated to English, Korean, Thai and many other international editions. As a painter, Mr. Liu has held more than thirty solo exhibitions throughout the world.

刘轩 Xuan Liu

音乐家、作家、演说家及主持人，美国哈佛
大学心理学硕士及博士研究生，目前致力于
在线教育，推广积极心理学。他也是受过古
典音乐训练的钢琴家和专业 DJ，拥有超过
25 年的音乐创作经验。出版作品十三部，包
括散文类、心理类和个人发展方面的书籍。

Writer, musician, lecturer, show host. Holds BA
from Harvard University and M.Ed from the
Harvard Graduate School of Education. He is also a
classically trained pianist and a professional DJ with
more than 25 years of experience. He has written
thirteen books, including essay collections and books
on psy— chology and personal development.

刘倚帆 Yvonne Liu

毕业于美国哥伦比亚大学及宾夕法尼亚大学沃顿
商学院研究所。目前在纽约从事科技行业，之前
在北京从事影视工作。出版英文翻译作品两种。

Holds BA from Columbia University and MBA from
the Wharton School of the University of Pennsylvania.
Currently based in NYC working in technology,
formerly based in Beijing as a film producer. Previously
translated two books from Chinese to English.

· 三位作者已经将本书在中国台湾的首版版税全数捐给台湾公益团体。细目见水云斋官网
（ syzstudio.com ）
  The author and translators have generously donated all royalties from the first printing
  to social and charitable causes.

索引
Indexes